Nothing In Moderation

A Biography
Of

ERNIE KOVACS

Nothing In Moderation

A Biography
Of

ERNIE KOVACS

by David G. Walley

Drake Publishers Inc

New York · London

Published in 1975 by
Drake Publishers, Inc.
381 Park Avenue South
New York, New York 10016

ISBN: 0-87749-738-9
LC: 74-22609

Book Design by Barry Eckstein

Printed in the United States of America.

Table of Contents

1   The Opening Credits/3
2   Stinky Water Notes/29
3   Dead Lion for Breakfast/57
4   Admit One (1) Passing Stranger/79
5   Miklos Molnar Meets Motzah Hepplewhite
      in the Big Apple/125
6   Eugene in Tinseltown/149
7   It's Been Real/205

Acknowledgements/222
Appendix/225
Television Background/240
Films of Ernie Kovacs/246

For my parents,
Miron and Silvia Walley

Type Casting

This is really a television script and not for radio at all. But as you will see the prospects of having it produced aren't very good. At the risk of seeming naive, I'll state that there is a slight problem of casting. You see, in the play I have definite views as to whom should play each part. The play is about movie stars and in the play I want Spencer Tracy to play a part called Marlon Brando. Marlon Brando to play a character called Walter Pigeon, who in turn, plays Cary Grant. And then for a complete circle, Cary Grant plays Spencer Tracy. In fact there's only one part in the whole play that doesn't present a casting problem. That's the part of Buzz Benson, a young television producer. The play is rather a play within a play. It begins, simply enough, at MGM studios in Buzz Benson's plush office. Everyone is there. Buzz speaks, "Gentlemen," he says, "what we got here is something. Really big." The movie stars murmer. Marlon Brando, who is really Spencer Tracy, replies, "I don't like it," he then undoes his shirt removes a glove from his pocket puts the glove on and scratches his stomach with his other hand. Walter Pigeon who is Marlon Brando says, "It smacks of deceit." No Cary Grant, played by Spencer Tracy, agrees with him. The young director is stymied. Cary Grant, Spencer Tracy in real life, then asks, "Who am I?" Marlon replies that, "If ya don't know, how d'ya expect-" Walter Pigeon says, "Well done Marlon." he then shakes the real Marlon Brando's hand, then embarassed by his mistake, he crosses quickly to Spencer tracy and says the line again. "Well done Marlon." now everybody laughs a little, but not enough to destroy empathy. Of course, this is easier to understand if you can picture it. *You see, all these stars are playing other big stars. What I'm trying to do in the play is to destroy type casting ... and I think I've done it.*

one page possibility by Ernie Kovacs
called Type Casting

THE OPENING CREDITS

It is Saturday night January 13, 1962 in Beverly Hills California on a typical Southern Californian winter's night. There is mist in the air, a fine rain is falling. A christening party is in progress in the apartment of Billy Wilder, the director, off the intersection of Wilshire Blvd and Beverly Glen. It could as easily be a gathering in West Covina or Hightstown, New Jersey, but here Milton Berle is being feted on the occasion of his newest son Michael, and all his Hollywood friends have come to wish him well. Dean Martin and Jeanie, his wife of the time, are there along with Yves Montand, Lucille Ball and her new husband Gary Morton, Jack Lemmon, director Dick Quine, and many, many others. This party has been going on for years at different houses in this community—nothing unusual here in this rarified community of stars, agents, producers and directors. They chat, smalltalk, drink their drinks and consume the catered Chassen's chili at yet another quiet evening away from the Biz and the glitter.

Also at this party is Ernie Kovacs, a large-framed, cigar-smoking television comedian who's been in Hollywood for the past five years pursuing a career in film. He's already done eight films, his newest, *Sail a Crooked Ship,* in which he plays a tippling, bumbling captain of a hijacked cargo ship is about to be released. There he meets his wife Edie Adams, the entertainer and musical comedy star, after spending a grueling day finishing up a television pilot for Screen Gems, a comedy western called *A Pony for Chris,* also featuring Buster Keaton. For the past three or four days he has been on a treadmill between the shooting and working on his seventh television special for Dutch Masters cigars where he has been directing, writing, and splicing tape constantly. He is tired, his bushy black eyebrows are weatherbeaten. His friends are concerned—those members of the 'Rat Pack," Jack Lemmon, Frank Sinatra, Dean Martin, Joey Bishop and the rest of the gang who've played many a hand of gin and stud poker in the outrageously opulent armorial den at Ernie's Coldwater Canyon home.

Kovacs seems to be his old wise-cracking self at the party while he regales his friends with tales of shooting a movie barechested in Griffith Park. He tells Jeanie Martin that he's going to live forever. How? "All it takes is three steam baths a day, lots of good brandy, about 20 cigars and work all night," he tells her. Normally he averages less than three hours of sleep a night if he sleeps at all. He is infamous in this crowd for hosting marathon poker games and gin parties in his steam room; king of the clubhouse. Jeanie is concerned about the steambaths' effect on his heart. "Look kid," he says, "this is the only life I've got and I want to live it the way I like! If I go, I want it to be my way...besides those steambaths don't hurt me, I can go all the time, day and night." He neglects to mention he's been living like that for 20 of his 42 years...he will be 43 in a week.

Kovacs has been a Puck figure ever since he came to Hollywood on the strength of a television special he did January of 1957, a silent show without dialogue but with plenty of sight gags and revolutionary camera tricks. Then Columbia Pictures offered him a large figure contract but recently he's been negotiating with Alec Guiness for a production deal and he's pleased with himself. For the first time since he's been here, he will have a chance to do what *he* wants. His Columbia deal didn't allow him to pick his own scripts. He's looking forward to exercising his creative freedom in a medium that has fascinated him for a long time.

The party ambles along until one o'clock and then Ernie decides to call it quits. He's going to PJ's, one of his hangouts on Santa Monica and Crescent Heights Boulevards in Hollywood to meet a friend for a nightcap and then home he tells his wife. The white Rolls which brought him to the party is outside along with the white Corvair stationwagon Edie drove down from the house. Since it's nasty outside and he's tired, he takes the wagon. He tells his wife to drive the other heap home. He's too tired to fight it any longer, so the compact is more maneuverable, especially in his condition.

On the way out he passes Yves Montand and asks him if he needs a lift to his hotel. No, Montand says. He's already promised Milton and Ruth Berle he'll ride with them...thanks just the same. Ernie waves goodbye and jumps into his car, sinking heavily into the cushions—the seatbelt remains unfastened as he wheels down Beverly Glen, heading towards Santa Monica and eventually east to PJ's.

The fine winter rain mist has made the roadway slick, water vapor mixing with the exhaust fumes on the heavily traveled road. The man with the big cigar and the big hands driving the cheaply constructed unstable rear-engine Corvair stationwagon is really too bushed to concentrate on his driving. It's a familiar enough route from Wilder's to PJ's anyway—the car just about drives itself, though a little too fast for the present conditions—whatthehell.

Ernie really isn't thinking about the road or his driving. He is meditating on the singular circumstances of his life: there's the money he owes the government, a cool $400,000, which if he can help it, they'll never see—fucking bloodsuckers forced him to make movies for $100,000 and then take 90...almost about to tag the furniture...just signed over $20,000 in government bonds which he'd been saving for his children. Then there are those IOU's that he's floated all over town incurred in the course of a bad run of Lady Luck, but he's sure the cards will change for him if he keeps at it...just one more hand. He's driving now through the Los Angeles Country Club grounds on the way to Santa Monica Blvd.

Time for a smoke, the twentieth or twenty-first of the day. He extracts from his jacket pocket another of those foot-long Havana specials, the baseball-bat specials which are his trademark, his obsession, and his pleasure. They line his pocket like bandoliers of ammunition. Fumbling for a kitchen match he attempts to strike it with his fingernail, a habit he picked up long ago (ya see the cigar's got to be caressed by the flame, just like a woman...lighters ruin the taste). In that split second as his car approaches the intersection, the wheels snag the concrete triangle ridges that intersect the meeting of Beverly Glen and Santa Monica. His fatigue-ridden senses over-compensate in braking. The vehicle starts to skid to the right, like some slow-motion stopaction movie, in a deathly parabola. His hands clutch the wheel in a frantic effort to steer through what will undoubtedly be a messy, final event. The unlit cigar is clasped between the first and second fingers of his right hand, with both hands on the wheel.

The white Corvair stationwagon with its revolutionary rear-engine displacement smashes broadside into the phone poles lining the road. Ernie is thrown to the other side of the front seat, buffeted by the force of the driver's door striking the poles. The passenger door springs open from the concussion as Ernie in shock, cigar still in hand, attempts to extricate himself from the twisted metal heap, heedless of the hairline fracture he's sustained when his head hit the steering wheel. In a last convulsive motion he manages to reach over the front seat in a futile crawl but dies. The unlit cigar drops from his hand and rests a few feet from his immobile body, just out of reach of his outstretched right arm.

Seconds later a young man who saw the accident take place pulls up to the scene. He's seen Kovacs on television and around in Beverly Hills, but he's too late to do anything for him. Dick Quine, Ernie's director on a few films and close personal friend, pulls up a few minutes later, having left Wilder's house a minute or so after Ernie. He is horrified—there is also nothing he can do now. The police arrive soon after and a crowd forms around the wreckage. Eventually the body is taken down to the morgue while the news spreads throughout the community and the news media. Quine calls Ed

Henry, Ernie's movie agent from MCA and between sobs tells him what has happened. Henry says he'll get over to Ernie's house right away and take care of Edie who still doesn't know what happened but will find out the next morning. Quine follows Henry to the house after leaving the scene of the accident.

Ernie's wife refuses to believe the horrible news until Jack Lemmon goes down to the morgue to verify the gruesome truth. "There he was, he was unmarked really, except under the hair...he looked very peaceful actually, almost smiling," said Lemmon. "It's typical of that sonofabitch that something would happen." Only then does Edie break down and is placed under sedation.

Sunday morning the crowds of the curious arrive before the gates of the Kovacs household in Coldwater Canyon and jostle each other like the premier scene from West's *Day of the Locust.* A Beverly Hills detective with whom Ernie used to ride on patrol duty from time to time tries to control the crowd before the agents, Marvin Moss and pr-man Henri Bollinger take charge, sorting out the friends from the ghoulish. Before they arrived Edie was answering the door every three seconds...a mobscene.

The funeral takes place four days later at the Beverly Hills Presbyterian Church on the corner of Santa Monica and Rodeo, a church Edie joined when she enrolled their children, Kippie and Betty, in Sunday school. It is attended by a varied multitude of the famous from Edward G. Robinson to Kim Novak to Jack Benny and Mary Livingston to Samuel Goldwyn to Buster Keaton to Charleton Heston. Edie wanted everybody and anybody that maybe knew Ernie or that Ernie respected to be there and they all came.

Ernie Kovacs was buried at Forest Lawn Cemetery in the Hollywood Hills. *Ernie Kovacs 1919-1962 Nothing in Moderation* read the epitaph on his simple stone. "He was one of those nuts that got to know everybody and everybody loved him," said friend Lemmon in tribute. Not only in Hollywood did they mourn, but wherever there were people who loved to laugh and use their vision as Kovacs had done, a vision where freedom was paramount, the freedom to laugh the cosmic laugh one more time.

Television in the late Forties and Fifties was essentially an experimental live medium—the mistakes you made were the mistakes the viewers saw. Part of the fun of Kovacs were the mistakes he made and the informality he lent to the medium before the advent of the slickness and the tape, the cost accountants and the censors. Television of the Fifties, where the newscasts were gray and the comedy was camp, was a collection of borscht belt routines and glitter, the drag-queen zaniness of Uncle Miltie which America avidly injested. Kovacs was not a Milton Berle nor a George Gobel nor a Red Skelton nor a Buster Keaton—though he had the wistful innocence of Chaplin and the off-color adlib wit of Groucho Marx. His scripts were never sacred—if there were any scripts to follow—and he wrote 9/10ths of his material himself. "Every idea I ever had is based on that fact that it's 2:30 and there's a production meeting at 3," he was fond of saying. Kovacs created most of his comedy in the heat of the moment when the beady little red eye of Camera One was on. Rather than scripts, he preferred visions—an automated office where the water cooler gurgled and the file cabinets sang like trumpets, a hand coming out of a bathtub to scrub the back of a pretty girl, the White Rock fairy taking a bath in the effervescent brook of gingeraleland. No one was immune.

Born with a cigar in his mouth and possibly a deck of cards in his hands, Kovacs' sardonic wit regularly lanced the banal. He was especially fond of poking fun at the bread-and-circus syndrome of daytime television quiz dramas. Like the show which he premiered once—briefly as it turned out—called "I've Got a Hush-Hush" where, like "I've Got a Secret," the guest came in to whisper his into the moderator's ear so that the viewing audience could be in on the fun. However, in Ernie's vision, the guest whispered his secret and then left. Neither the audience, nor the panelists ever found out what the 'hush-hush' was. Blackout.

One asks at this point, if these are the shows, what can the game be like? There was another game he played a few times called "Whom Done It?" where a panelist and possibly the home viewing audience was supposed to guess what crime a contestant had committed...but nothing was ever that simple especially the rules:

> If our astute panel members fail to guess whom done it, the contestant will receive many wonderful prizes unless he has used a sentence in answering the questions which ends with a preposition, in which case he not only will not receive any prizes, but must contribute equal and same prizes to each of the panelists, with one exception. That should one of the panelists use a question containing a double negative, he or she will have to change clothes with someone in the audience and will lose his turn on the panel for the remainder of that round. Unless the person with whom he changes clothing is seated in the third seat of the fourth row, in which case, it will be the person immediately to the right of the person in the audience who will change clothes with the losing panelist. There now...I think all of the rules are clear and here's how we play "Whom Done It?"

To today's sophisticated viewers, these ancient rules sound

complex and even silly, actually parodied, but "Whom Done It?" was no sillier than any number of shows that appeared on daytime television in the Fifties and survive in part today. Television in the Fifties with minor exceptions was a selling medium for soap, suppositories, and status—a medium of control with hour upon hour of smiling emcees parading human misery and greed. Kovacs for all his levity and jokes about the stupidity of television was deeply committed to making it into truly an adult medium instead of a haven for 12-year-old minds.

Near the height of his popularity he wrote in a LIFE Magazine cover story, an article on the subject, "The television audience of today is a sophisticated, alert, discriminating audience, quick to reject the inadequate. The picture of a nationwide audience holding its sides in ecstatic empathy as a smiling young man runs up and down the aisles kissing old ladies and handing out orchids to grandmothers is one that has been removed to the attic, along with the kinescopes of those programs." He believed that in the end it was the networks which would have to bend— "the networks to maintain and create further great programming accomplishments, will have to compromise their cost-accounting system."

But in the end, it was the cost-accounting system which contributed to Ernie's financial ruin when he was producer of his own television specials. The omniscient studio accountant knew little of theater and less of television production, especially Ernie's way. Thus the estimated cost of Ernie's first Dutch Masters special for April, 1961, was $11,174.00. It became $25,185.83 by showtime. Budgeted rehearsal time was 12 hours on paper; actually it was more like 25 hours. The final tag included an additional $5,000 for production penalties as well as double and triple overtime for the crews, since Ernie believed in continuity of action. In real terms that meant long hauls of 24-to-30 hours straight. There's a fairly well substantiated rumor around the ABC-television lot in Hollywood that many of his technicians are driving around in Cadillacs due to Ernie's spend-it-like-water theories of labor.

He was ahead of his time in the field of television comedy in the Fifties. He had a stableful of characters—the infamous Percy Dovetonsils; the inscrutable Charlie Clod, Charlie Chan's left-handed cousin; Irving Wong, the Chinese songplugger; and Wolfgang Sauerbraten, the all-night German disk-chockey, a distinguished gray-maned gentlement with lederhosen and an atrocious Hollywood German accent:

Guttenack, klina fraulines, fraus und herrs...dine disk chockey, Wolfgang Sauerbraten moosiks du liebe...klina liebshan, dise nacht we blay zom heis moosiks let ein spreighen de newest b-bopper...du dist the moch greunadawn veather...
spreighen enima lina b-bopper ish der ben cool dis nacht un crazy en morgen...eh? ich weiss nich was is sogen...un laben, leichen, en spreichet ein commercial

closing with, of course a word from the sponsor:

Ach, sich shoen blamieran. Ich musten eilen. es suspat. Ich haben hayben musten spreichen gutton nachte. Un remindun, davega storen, feer dreis 42 strasse, binb bomb tables, catcher mitts und hockey shticks...gutten nachte aus Wolfgang Sauerbraten, du all nachen disk chockey.

All pure ad-lib, Kovacs just got into costume and into character on camera. A born mimic, he made any accent (including his native Hungarian) his own and used it with mirthful intent like the commercial for Colonel Janos Kentucky Fried Paprikas. Only in the world of Ernie Kovacs could there be such a creature as a Kentucky Hungarian speiling the following shtick:

Us Kentucky Hungarians know yo' folks is sick of a-fussin' ovah youah paprikas. So us Kentucky Hungarians figgered yo' like to know whuts on the inside...
(close up of soup spoon with one ping pong ball in it)
"A nice, round potato, home grown to puffection on a Kentucky lathe...
(cross dissolve to c.u. of toothpick with 3 peas stuck on it)
3 rich green peas grown in dark brown Budapest gravy and deep fat fried to pufect excellence...and the whole mess of rich, deep-lovin' goodness is fricassed fo' elebem hours...

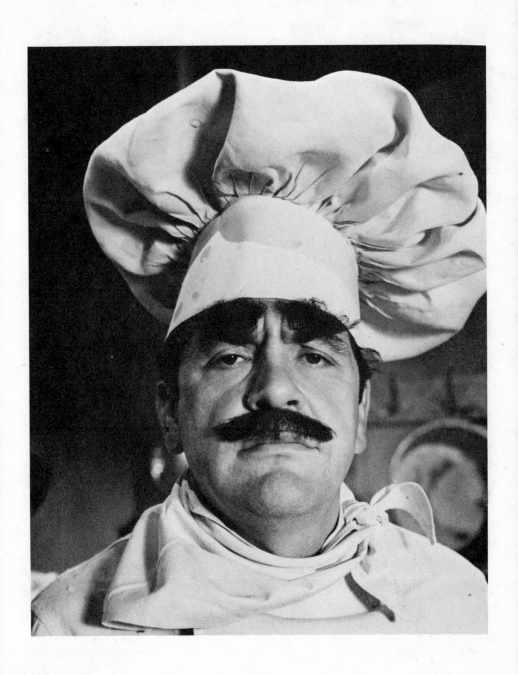

(cross dissolve to c.u. of bottle labeled Kentucky Budapest Bourbon)
in solid 180 proof Kentucky Budapest Bourbon.
So, as old Sam Janos used to say---and remembah - Make sure it's Janos.

And of course there were his cheapo epic films, parodies of late-night television reruns...cheap because much of the time in his early days, he never had a budget for the props he needed. Hence the silent movie treatment: a roller jerkily unfolds the credits:

IVBAN TROO DE MILL PRESENTS
A TALE OF ESPIONAGE
UNDERCOVER GOINGS ON IN A RESTAURANT
COLD CUTS OF STEEL IN HOTBEDS OF SPIES
RANSACKED RADAR
HIJACKED HYDROGEN
PILFERED PEROXIDE
BOY!
SEE SNEAKY SPIES AT WORK
SEE UNCLE SAM STRIKE BACK
SEE THE CHARGE OF WILD BULL ELEPHANTS
SWOLLEN RIVERS
THE DYNAMITING OF HOOVER DAM (NARTB)
WITH A CAST OF A FEW!
SEE HEADLESS HEROINES
ON THE STRETCHOMATIC SCREEN!
WITH SCHIZOPHRENIC SOUND!
IN GLORIOUS GRAYS AND BLACKS!
AS TOLD TO IVBAN TROO DE MILL BY A FORMER IRISH SPY!
WE ARE INDEBTED TO THE F.B.I. FOR THE LOAN OF
THEIR TYPEWRITER WITHOUT WHICH THIS SCRIPT

WOULD NOT HAVE BEEN POSSIBLE
THE CAST IN THE ODOR OF THEIR AP-
PEARANCE
ARCHDUKE O'TOOLE...MANNY SHEVITZ
CAROUSEL TICKET COLLECTOR...BUSHMASTER
KREEL
LADY PAMELA MAINWARING...BESSIE LOU
COSNOWSKI
THE HOODED STRANGER...LISTERINE GOLD-
FARB
USED GONDOLA SALESMAN...CORDELLA
PFUNF
ELDERLEY MAN..."WHITEY" GROOTZ
THE CHINESE COOK...SIR BRADFORD
SHULTZ
AND INTRODUCING
MOISCH!

Just as silent movies, typed cards would convey whatever cheapo action would occur. In keeping with the loose nature of an Ivban Troo De Mill production, the cue cards could be fawled...er flawed:

MEANWHILE...BACK AT TRADER LOUIE'S, THE HOODED STRANGER WAS AP-PRIE...APPREHENSN...NERVOUS

Since nothing was ever that easy in Kovacsland, the silent movie endings were slightly deranged parodies sometimes combined with Gilbert and Sullivan cases of mistaken identity (as if anyone knew what was going to happen), which produced (at long last!) a denouement remotely like this for the aforementioned spectacular:
DIALOGUE: AH HAH! I HAVE CAUGHT YOU, SPY
     NO. 2.
   action: Sandy [Stewart, a Kovacs regular in 1953] whips off
       disguise...shows badge on chest...speaks

DIALOGUE: NO, I AM A FEMALE UNITED STATES
DEPUTY MARSHALL...*HERE* IS YOUR SPY.

action: Sandy points to Andy [McKay, another Kovacs regular]...Andy whips off disguise...has similar star...speaks

DIALOGUE: NO, I TOO AM A UNITED STATES
DEPUTY MARSHALL...THERE IS YOUR SPY!

action: Andy points to ko[vacs]...ko whips off disguise...points to his badge

DIALOGUE: OH NO, LIKEWISE, I AM A UNITED
S T A T E S   D E P U T Y   MAR-
SHALL...THEN...TRADER LOUIE'S SON
MUST BE THE SPY!

action: all point to Trig ger Lund)...he rips off disguise...speaks

DIALOGUE: AU CONTRAIRE, FELLOW UNITED
STATES DEPUTY MARSHALS, I TOO AM A
UNITED STATES DEPUTY MARSHALL...

action: ko hits self on head...speaks

DIALOGUE: AND WE HAVE BEEN FOLLOWING
EACH OTHER FOR ELEVEN YEARS FOR
NOTHING!

action: all begin to choke each other.

DIALOGUE: THIS FILM WAS ACTUALLY FILMED
IN A RESTAURANT ONCE OWNED BY A MAN
WHOSE NEIGHBOR WAS A UNITED STATES
DEPUTY MARSHALL.

The viewers in Kovacsland were used to this...they expected it; what other show would allow it...what other network? Really none of them after awhile. What could an advertisement for Harmon Guggenflekker's Quick Frozen Noodnicks be like? or Lost Beer? Kovacs' shows were possibly the only time on television where absolutely no one took anything seriously, and there were always bits which were light on scenery but heavy on imagination. Like the Uncle Gruesome puppet show which sometimes appeared...*sometimes.* Uncle Gruesome was a nice old man who

told horrid fairy tales for horrid little boys and girls...horridly if one can make an adhominum judgement here:

Well...here we are again boys and girls...you remember last week we left our story in the old mouldy cave in the haunted mountain. The three-eyed gargoyle had just made a big pot of dead bat stew, when someone knocked at the door with a human hip bone. Well boys and girls, the gargoyle's two-headed pet pussycat meooed twice, once for each child. The rotting door burst open and twelve crazy elephants with green trunks and bloody fangs ran into the kitchen. (Gruesome looks in opposite direction of cue cards hastily)...Whoops, here comes that old grouch again, time to go, but remember Auntie Gruesome will be back next Tuesday brought to you by that wonderful breakfast food that is partially shot from guns, Hot Noodnicks!

That was the point as well with Ernie's humor, he would go to any lengths to get a laugh. Some of his friends thought that was his weakness—better writers, editing they thought. But Ernie never used his writers that much. When he finally came to Hollywood in 1957 and set up his den, he came into contact with the rest of his peers in the comedic tradition. He was good friends with all the vaudeville refugees, especially Groucho Marx, though his form of humor eluded them. The inscrutable Jack Benny said to Ernie during a dressing room conversation, "I don't know what it is about you. I watch, I listen, I laugh."

He had few echoes—one of the few performers whose off-and on-of camera lives coincided—and he certainly had style. He spent an estimated $13,000 per year on special Havana cigars, and he offered you one almost as soon as he met you as a sign of friendship. He was the type of man who if he liked you wanted to include you in all his activities, a trip to the poker table, or the steamroom. And if Ernie was associated with cigars throughout his lifetime, he was certainly associated with cards which he played with a passion bordering on a mania. He was an enthusiastic if unlucky gambler, the type of player who would beat you to death with money...even a pair of deuces. If his bluff failed he'd say, "Gee, too bad...I thought I had you there." Occasionally he'd win big, like $48,000 in one Hollywood poker game pulling two cards to an inside straight. But that was pure luck and he lost much more than he could ever win. He was such an enthusiastic and obsessed gambler that he'd call you up in the middle the night, "Come on down, we need a fourth...honest," and you'd go because you loved him, because it was Ernie. You went even if you had to drag your four-year-old son into the city and have him sleep on the porch while you played. You went.

Kovacs lived magnificently, splendidly, if you will. The best of everything, big cars with telephones in the back, "I'm approaching Beverly Glen dear, make sure the martinis are iced" ... an intimate of the Stork Club (rest in peace) and Sardi's in New York, the Rat Pack in Hollywood. Once he ran up a $7,000 tab in Sardi's in the mid-Fifties and when he was asked why he continued to patronize the restaurant, he characteristically replied, "Look if I don't go in there, he's going to ask me for the money." That makes a certain kind of sense, but only if you were Ernie Kovacs. He lived for the moment. His most famous words uttered, during a Cuban invasion rehearsal in 1961, to his longtime crony and director Barry Shear were characteristic. The government was closing in on him for back taxes. They'd already squirreled him into a 95-plus-5 percent bracket and were forcing him to work just for them. It was the type of hock that you don't easily escape. When the sirens wailed, they both thought it was curtains. Ernie turned to Barry and said, "I did it, I did it! I fucked the government out of $400,000 dollars." One can only admire such pluck in times of adversity.

But that wasn't funny really, it was one of the unfunniest threads of Kovacs' life. He'd joke about it, used to say to his friends when the burden was more 'manageable,' "There's nothing that $80,000 couldn't cure." It was a fact of his life, the goad. He spent water like money...er money like water—probably would have spent water like water too if he could of figgered a way to transport it. He couldn't resist the grand gesture, and when he got to Hollywood which was already filled with big spenders and big tippers, Ernie just couldn't stand to be outdone. He was famous for picking up checks out there...he was famous back in his hometown of Trenton, New Jersey...the easiest touch in town, people would line up for blocks just to ask Ernie for money.

Money was a tool, a kick, a gesture—it didn't mean anything. It was fun. He earned it, dammit, he'd spend it. Only Kovacs would have a wine cellar built into his basement with a phony Jack Benny-type combination lock and thick heavy bolts. Only Ernie would wire the special effects department at ABC to spray fake cobwebs on the bottles. "Wanna take a look at the winecellar?" Creeeeek, "the Chateau Lafitte Rothchild is rather good...want a bottle...want a case?" What else was it good for anyway? Either you spent it quick or the government spent it for you on some war or porkbarrel scheme—flood reparations for indigent chukkers in

South Hampton or more security fences at San Clemente.

Once Ernie came to New York with his whole family—his wife Edie and children Kippie and Betty, plus a maid to do a guest spot for some television extravaganza. He rented a suite of rooms at the Plaza with room service included, natch. Along about the end of the first week, Ernie discovered that his fee for doing the show would be considerably less than the hotel bill. Ernie put his foot down—*any* husband, any right thinking American living in the Plaza has to see reality once in a while. He decreed after much thought that the whole brood would have to take meals at stated time. Well, at least that would cut down on the room service.

Hollywood changed him...slightly. His poker buddies and gin schnorrer cronies may have been Jack Lemmon or Billy Wilder or Tony Curtis or Edward G. Robinson, but he still had time for his crews, his partners in crime. One of the most unusual aspects of Ernie's lifestyle was his ability to communicate with everyone. In Hollywood the "talents" rarely if ever condescend to mingle socially with the technicians, the cyphers who do the dirty work. Next to writers they were the lowest on the social scale...but not to Ernie. He encouraged them to be as creative as possible on set, and off-set encouraged them to visit his home and try their luck at cards (if they had any money) or just hang out.

One cameraman Bob Kemp, who was also Ernie's staff photographer for "Take a Good Look", an off-the-wall quiz program, brought by some photos one afternoon. Ernie asked him in for a drink.

"Vodka and..." Bob hesitated for a moment.

"You like vodka," said Kovacs, "just a sec." He opened the freezer in his den and extracted a glass hoary with frost as well as a bottle of liquid potato. He poured a healthy shot into the glass and said, "Drink this."

Bob was a little surprised and hesitated, taking a small pull.

"No," said Kovacs jovially, "pour it right down," and he helped Bob pour it right down, setting the poor man on fire. Not content with one, Ernie insisted on a refill, pouring himself one in the process. Within an hour's time they'd killed half the bottle, just for the hell of it, because it was there to be drunk and enjoyed.

Kovacs was a walking paradox, a huge framed man over six-feet tall, with even larger hands, who had the mind of a precocious adolescent whose wistful innocence enveloped him like an aura. He was super machismo, prone to swear with love and determination but was also gentle, kind and sensitive. For all his openness, he was an elusive figure—man of a thousand faces and places.

He came to Hollywood expecting to be received on the strength of his television work, to be allowed to innovate as he'd done on television and radio for the past 17 years in Philadelphia and New York. He discovered there the agony of working within a system where the creative urge was regimented by the enforced segregation of writers, producers, and directors gummed together by agents of all kinds. Hollywood, where if you were cast for a role you stayed with it.

So Ernie became THE CAPTAIN for Hollywood and ever after, the comedic para-military villain: Captain Lock in *Operation Madball,* Captain Segurra in *Our Man in Havana,* Captain Stark in *Wake Me When It's Over,* The Captain in *Sail a Crooked Ship.* At one point Ernie took out an ad in Hollywood Variety, "No more @#/+# Captains," it read. Ed Henry his movie agent from MCA tried to explain, "I argued the point with Ernie that in the period when he was coming on he wouldn't be considered a star because in those days we still had the 'handsome-good-looking', so-called, look. It was always my feeling with Ernie that he was a personality, rather than a romantic image. In Hollywood, if you wanted a romantic image, then you had to hold the picture, and if the picture was a failure, you were a failure." You are what you project.

In all, Kovacs was an American original who possessed a cockeyed world vision augmented by silence..."Eugene." On January 19, 1957, Kovacs thrilled the NBC television audience with an unexpected half hour show, a filler for a Jerry Lewis show. Kovacs, who was hired at the last minute, instead of playing it safe thought to innovate television by presenting an entirely silent, no-dialogue show. The major portion concerned the trials and tribulations of Eugene, a schnook dressed in a Norfolk jacket who wandered into a stuffy men's club. Eugene was a cockeyed everyman, a victim of society who nevertheless kept his good nature in spite of circumstances definitely beyond his control. He succeeded despite the fact that his shoes squeaked when he walked, that when eating his gauche box lunch his celery stalks sounded like splitting trees. His thermos coffee poured at a 15⁰ angle to his cup, olives snaredrummed down the dining room table. Eventually he righted the table throwing the members off skew.

Eugene in many ways was the inverted Kovacs, his foil. If any of Ernie's characterizations were closest to him and most beloved by his fans, it was Eugene with his sense of wonder and innocence in the face of civilized barbarities.

Possibly Ernie would have liked and enjoyed the type of epic where the scantily clad maidens are throwing rose petals in front of his sedan chair, where the valet in woven gold toga is carrying a golfbag filled with cigars, where the Jack Daniels or Wild Turkey in ice is held aloft as he is marched majestically towards the golden sunset. He also might have opened this book like this:

Opening Shot

Full length -- of two apes...one sitting in chair cigar in mouth with derby, white breakaway vase in hand...other has on black beret seated at typewriter...obviously he is writing something about other ape. *Sound:* electric typewriter

Titles Roll -- while on titles, apes move to another spot...the ape at typewriter is surrounded by ticker-tape up to waist...positions are unchanged.

Back to Apes -- writer ape...spreads arms in dismay, other ape with cigar and derby hits writer ape on head with vase...writer ape whips out submachine and riddles other ape...note: no one falls down...both stare at viewer...

Strangely Believe It!

PICTURES BY WALLACE WOOD

CONTRARY TO POPULAR OPINION,

WAVING A RED FLAG AT A BULL

DOES NOT IRRITATE HIM!

ACTUALLY **COWS** ARE THE ONES WHO GET IRRITATED WHEN A RED FLAG IS WAVED AT THEM.

The reason a BULL gets mad when a RED FLAG is waved at him is because he dislikes being mistaken for a COW.

BULL DURHAM

KEEP OUT

POST NO BULLS

ARMAND K. FRECHETTE

A FUR TRAPPER from GRANDEBOUCHE Canada,

TRAPPED A **SINGLE MINK** WORTH **$8000.⁰⁰**

IT WAS DRAPED OVER THE BACK OF A CHAIR AT THE STORK CLUB.

Although a pound of **SALAMI** and a pound of **LIVERWURST** weigh **EXACTLY THE SAME,** THREE POUNDS of **CHOPPED LIVER** weighs more than both put together.

ARTHUR K. LIMBISH

a little known **COMEDY WRITER** MEMORIZED THE TAG LINES FOR OVER **930,000** JOKES THE REASON ARTHUR IS A LITTLE KNOWN COMEDY WRITER IS HE NEVER LEARNED THE SET-UP LINES.

JOE MILLF

THE FANTASTIC ODDS OF

10,000 TO ONE

WERE LEVELED AGAINST "FIREBRAND"

WINNING THE EPSOM DOWNS DERBY STEEPLECHASE IN 1938

AXOLOTL DAILY BLEH
SATELLITE IMPOSSIBLE SAYS RUSSIAN SCIENTIST
WAR TO BE

Daily Tout and Tipster

"FIREBRAND" WAS A GARTER SNAKE.

ALTHOUGH THE **MOON** IS ONLY **ONE 49TH** THE SIZE OF THE **EARTH,** IT IS **FURTHER AWAY!**

A MAN TRAVELLING ON FOOT FROM **TOKYO,** JAPAN, TO **SAN DIEGO,** CALIFORNIA

... WILL **DROWN** BEFORE HE GOES A HUNDRED MILES!

19

**Pioneer . . . early American who was lucky enough to find his way out of the woods.

Stinky Water Notes

2

"...He wasn't too highly regarded around...he wasn't what you'd call a hippie, a hippie type, but he was not a serious settled guy—and he was in a new industry, or trying to get into it...the theater which was not regarded with too much respect as a place for an ambitious young man to be and when he started to get into television and things like that it was sort of a crazy idea. I remember Alex Segel's father who had a delicatessen on Market Street telling me how terrible it was for Alex to be working in television instead of getting a job teaching."

'common sense' from Trenton, New Jersey
"We instinctively dislike a tall, heavy man with a mustache. This description applies most specifically to us. When we see us approaching in a mirror, until we recognize the face, we get our dander up. When we see who it is, it's worse."

Kovacs on Kovacs in *The Trentonian*

The student director of Trenton High's 1936 production of Gilbert and Sullivan's *"HMS Pinafore"* is frazzled on account of clown in the chorus, an ex-preppy named Ernie Kovacs. Not only are his imitations of the director's mannerisms and speech patterns devastatingly accurate, they are undermining his authority! (Student directors tend to take themselves seriously.) In desperation he calls in the chairman of the drama department, 'Van' Kirk, a man so imposing and theatrical that he can make the Yellow Pages sound like Hamlet—he'll shut down this character with wildhorse eyes who's bubbling over with pure mischief.

While the young apprentice is out, the chorus relaxes, but when the door opens and Van appears with his assistant, there is silence. With a slow measured tread Van stalks over to Kovacs as the chorus parts, the Red Sea before the fiery pillar of God's retribution. Van halts before the offender and taking him by the lapels pulls him down to eye level, asking him in a low voice so as not to cause further disturbance,

"Do you like being in the show?"

"Yes," Kovacs replies in a similarly low tone.

"Are you sure," reinterates Van.

"Remember...one more word and you're *OUT!*"

Thereafter Kovacs does as he's told. The rehearsal is saved and the show is a success.

****

This young troublemaker has already been through an unsettled childhood before locking horns with the imperious Kirk. The youngest of the Kovacs brood, next to brother Tom, Ernie was born January 19, 1919, and has known a variety of financial and emotional circumstances. Both his parents are strong-willed. Andrew, his father, a heavyset boisterous man known as a ladykiller around town has been a foot patrolman on the Trenton police force, a failed bootlegger, and now runs a small restaurant in town. His idea of a good time is to hire an organ grinder to play on the police chief's lawn at 3 AM. A tough man, he had emigrated from Hungary at 13. Ernie's mother, Mary, is a handsome woman with a rich laugh and gifted seamstress fingers. She is fiercely proud of her youngest and is constantly at odds with her husband. He and his brother become experts at disappearing into the woodwork when the grownups have a go at each other. As a child, Ernie's favorite trick is to draw footprints all over his bedroom ceiling which finally lead out the window to freedom.

As his mother's favorite, Ernie has already received more than his share of attention, which leads to some embarrassing moments growing up on Clinton Street in the less prosperous southside of Trenton. His mother's doting fingers once made him a marvellous black velvet Lord Fauntleroy suit at which the neighborhood youths took umbrage. In Ernie's words, "it was like walking around with a sign that said 'kick me.' When I went outside I came running home with ten guys chasing me. I had to make up for it by playing on three different baseball teams." Mary also feeds him to death. "The baseball helped me lose weight too. My mother was one of those parents who thinks a child isn't healthy unless he's buttered in fat. For a long time, I looked like a balloon."

A spoiled fat little boy, Ernie first experienced a change in the family fortunes at ten when his father, taking advantage of his connections on the force (as well as Trenton's appetite for softdrinks) became a 'beverage dealer' during prohibition. The family moves into the Parkside section of town to a 20-room mansion complete with stables, kennels and a four-car garage. Ernie even has his own pony.

Because of good fortune, Ernie is placed in Miss Bowen's Private School, where his naturally inquisitive mind devours knowledge rapidly. He takes part in two plays in elementary school—one, the lead in Old King Cole. His mother to celebrate that event makes a special trip to Philadelphia to a professional costumer much to the chagrin of the teachers at the Parkside School who have to work hard to match her son's finery with their cheesecloth. Her interest in her son's career isn't strictly limited to theater either—she also outfits the whole eighth-grade baseball team with new uni-forms—an idyllic time.

All comes to a shattering end when Andrew's business bottoms out in 1935. Gone the mansion and the pony, and Ernie who has already skipped two grades enters Trenton High as a junior who though bright is bored with public school academics. An indifferent student slated to graduate in 1936, he is held back another semester to make up failures in history, latin, algebra, and first-semester chemistry. He continues to have an abiding interest in theater, coupled with a splendid baritone voice which leads him to join the chorus for the *Pinafore,* where he has his fateful meeting with Van.

In the fall of 1937, Ernie returns to THS for post-graduate work and again joins the chorus, now doing *The Pirates of Penzance.* He briefly makes friends with the accompanist, Eddie Hatrak, also a post graduate with whom he will work a few years later on Trenton's local radio station WTTM. Hatrack eventually goes to Julliard and doesn't return to Trenton until 1941.

Since Ernie has distinguished himself admirably in *Pinafore,* Van feels he would do well in the role of the Pirate King; Ernie already has the requisite *chutzpah* but lacks confidence. The matter is broached in characteristic delicacy:

"Do you sing?"

"No, not really," replied Ernie.

"Never say it," replied Van, "as of now, you *SING.*"

Ernie would use that rationale many, many times in his future work.

The *Pirates* proves an even greater triumph for Ernie, even though he thought he couldn't sing, and Van encouraged by Ernie's natural ability when asked to direct at the John Drew Memorial Theater in Easthampton, Long Island, manages to secure a full scholarship for his prize pupil. A full summer of walk-ons, supporting roles, second leads, Ernie appears in *Green Grow the Lilacs, Stage Door, The Frogs,* and second lead in *Arms and the Man* for which he receives his first bad notice—a critic called him a ham. "All that remark shows is that critics aren't as smart as they should be," notes Van. "Ernie never overacted, but his personality was such that he simply overpowered everybody, even in a small part. He couldn't have played it down, it wouldn't have been Ernie." And Van already knew.

During that summer, Ernie also learns other aspects of the actor's lot. He enthusiastically participated in the interminable post-curtain poker games and watched cityslicker actors, who kept notebooks of their winnings, clean him out night after night. Ernie had been playing poker since 11, but more than once during his stint in summer stock, he lost his week's salary to fill a straight flush in draw poker and then bet against someone else's full house.

In the fall of 1937, again through the good offices of Van, he receives a scholarship from the American Academy of Dramatic Arts in New York. His circumstances in Trenton were mean but livable-New York became an unspeakable ordeal. He moves into a $4-a-week room in a fifth-floor walkup on West 74th Street and is still naive enough to be shocked when his landlady and some of her 'daughters' are busted for running a whorehouse directly below his room. He is so poor that he can barely afford a loaf of bread a day, forget the margarine. And if he wants a hot meal, he heats up water, drops the bread in and makes gruel. Obviously he learned firsthand about Nedicks with 'it's real citris-aid atmosphere, the combination cream cheese and peanut butter sandwich for a nickel, the seven cent coffee all washed down with a large free clean glass of water.'

When he tired of gruel and the Lemon Room, Ernie would starve himself for a few days to save up 35 cents for a night out: a 20-cent plate of spaghetti (with a nickel tip) and a movie. He had to move quickly by crosstown bus, for the poverty flickers—his chosen theater—charged 10 cents before seven o'clock. At those prices he never expected much, "Usually it was the life of Beethoven," remembered Ernie later on and further away, "I saw that seven times."

Memories of those scuffling days survived in Ernie's cheapo spectaculars for radio and television:

"YES, PASSIONATA IS THE MOVING STORY OF A PIANIST AND HIS FATHER WHO WAS A PIANOMOVER. PASSIONATA WILL MAKE YOU

GASP WITH FEAR...YOU'LL GASP WHEN
LITTLE AMADEUS TREBLECLEFF FIGHTS
THE TWO INSANE CHINESE LAUNDRYMEN
WHEN THEY FEED THE POISONED LICHEE
NUTS TO HIS PET MONGOOSE."

It wasn't the grinding poverty which nagged him as much as not knowing what really to do with himself—even the busses cost money, and once you'd been to all the free entertainment, what was left? Not the most gracious view of New York by a longshot. He returned briefly to Trenton for some Depression theatrics, before another summer in Easthampton in 1938. The second year at the American Academy, his health began to fail from the poverty regimen, and the following summer when Ernie was working in Vermont, he collapsed, stricken with pleurisy complicated by pneumonia. All those latenight poker games and malnutritioned spaghetti dinners, plus the five flights to the left had taken their toll. Even if Ernie wanted to return home, there was no home to speak of—his parents had separated, and he found himself on Welfare Island where he began what he later called "The Welfare Island Engagement," in the terminal ward close to death.

Better than theater it was. Ernie wound up performing daily and nightly to enthusiastic audiences of doctors and patients. He was once wheeled into the flouriscope room for a routine examination of his lungs, but when the attendant switched on the lamps, neatly stenciled on his chest in aluminum were the words, "Out to Lunch." And though he always looked like he was a candidate for Potter's Field, he kept the staff amused. He organized checker tournaments for left-handed players with three or more gallstones, poker games for anemics whose pulse could break a hundred, all in an effort to beat the reaper.

The ward in which Ernie first resided contained about a hundred beds, and being a newcomer to the ward, he was placed near the door though he was always angling for a window seat and a bit of sky. As he inexorably moved toward the window through the attrition of his peers, he gradually became aware of the sound of carpenters working outside the window. Good-o, at least he'd see some life even if he couldn't be there himself quite yet. When he finally reached a windowbed and looked out, he learned that indeed carpenters were at work, but not building houses...COFFINS! There were dozens piled against the wall. Ernie put his face against the glass and hollered as loud as he dared, *"Which one has my name on it!!"*

"All the time I was supposed to be dying—the only thing the docs couldn't figure out was why I didn't hurry up about it."

Quoth E.

He would have probably been thrown out of Welfare Island for malingering if it had not been for the timely intervention of Van, who returning to the States in 1940 after a sabbatical leave in England, arranged for Ernie's transfer to a sanitorium in Browns Mills, New Jersey. Through a subscription raised by other friends, Ernie received a radio to wile away the hours as well as a small allowance. He read copiously and the money no doubt went to poker while the radio stayed tuned to WQXR, a New York City classical music station. Between the cadenzas, Ernie entered and won many radio contests.

Though Browns Mills was closer to home and in a less depressing environment, Ernie still rebelled against hospital restrictions. They had forbidden him to smoke cigars which would only damage his tender lungs. Albeit they were less than concerned that he was utterly devoted to the habit since age 16. They didn't smoke anyway, how would they know what 'not smoking' was...like the sound of one hand clapping? Andrew, as any good father, smuggled into his son the precious tobacco tubes—hell with them! Some basketcase, he'd been hospitalized for nearly 18 months by early 1941, when the hunting season approached. If the doctors were concerned about his smoking one can imagine how they would have reacted to his walking. But Ernie didn't ask them. Andrew came to the rescue again and smuggled a shotgun suitable for small game. At the earliest possible moment, Ern slipped out, pajamas under raincoat, and into the woods for a solitary shooting day in the southern New Jersey scrub. The staff never knew.

A few weeks later one of the doctors told him that since his recovery was progressing so splendidly he might be able to join the other clinging vines on the front lawn for some sun.

"Gee that's great," said Ernie innocently enough.

'Twas neither Dame Nicotine nor the call of the wild which finally persuaded Kovacs to terminate his engagement at Browns Mills. A far more primitive urge compelled him—*Kovachior, Kovachior*--Cincinatus from the plow. Early in the summer of 1941, he took french leave of the sanitorium, deserting for the footlights. Perhaps he would make some money though more importantly he wanted to live again in front of the lights.

Hardly what one could call first-rate theater really, rather a shyster producer from Phillie with a big car and a flashy blond enticed Kovacs from his bed of pain with a hundred-dollar retainer. Such a simple deal—he wouldn't kid him—in exchange for a percentage of the house. Ernie would be the chief actor/director/producer and bottlewasher for the Contemporary Players, a pickup dramatics group composed of Trenton High alumni. Ernie and the producer would split a percentage while the crew took the sparechange...why not?

They booked themselves into the Contemporary Club in downtown Trenton, an edifice long since destroyed by flames (though it could as easily have been the irate cast of *Dark Victory,* heir first production). The kids sold tickets like bucketshop professionals; it was all so professional that the night of the performance, the producer from Philadelphia ran off with the receipts leaving Kovacs and crew holding the bucket. Rumor had it that Ernie himself was in on the job and split the boodle. No way. The Contemporary Players for the duration of the summer season of 1941 fast became the *Compulsory* Players ...quickly. They owed everybody: Samuel

French, the gas company, the costumer, the printer. Ernie was back in Trention alright...back in hock.

But it was theater, no matter how strawhat, and it was experience—boy! Ernie was indeed the whole show with moderate assistance. He played all the leads, directed, assembled the incidental music from his record collection, changed the lights when necessary and scouted properties. He improvised with public-domain works, turning them into plays. But in characteristic fashion he never managed to write out the third acts so each time they were performed they were different. According to his associates at the time, his tastes in props veered toward schlock realism. In his production of Thorton Wilder's *Our Town,* he substituted a real coffin for the imaginery one that Wilder had in mind for the graveyard scene, no doubt drawing on his fresh experiences at Welfare Island. Thank you, no. During that summer he was never short of stagestruck girl-friends for female leads. His one platonic girlfriend, Edna Vine, was a case study in frustration (they never made it because they both laughed too much). Just when it appeared she would finally get a lead, Ernie found another actress.

The Contemporary Players worked throughout the greater Trenton area with gusto. No house was too modest, no audience too small. They played Dr. Jeckyl and Mr. Hyde in Bordontown, and after the first two lines Ernie heard echoes in the high school auditorium. He looked out and counted exactly four people. When he asked them whether they wanted refunds, the four were adamant—they'd come to see the production and they demanded continuance. So much for nohat theater.

By season's close, dreams of glittergelt and Broadway openings faded. The grandiose proceeds, less assumed debts, was one string of Christmas lights which Ernie had donated to the company previously as a gift. Reality intruded itself and Ernie returned to his mother's house over a candystore—two rooms divided by a curtain, in front of which Mary plied her trade as a seamstress. As poor as she was, she always managed to feed her son proper food—Charlotte Russe and steak. Afterward Ernie always maintained that he'd rather eat Charlotte Russe and steak one night and starve the other six than eat hamburger seven nights...it figured.

He next took a job in a drugstore in Princeton, New Jersey, to help out at home. Beside commuting an hour by car, Kovacs-style (meaning in practical terms barrelassing over county roads at breakneck speed), the job required a certain amount of physical exertion—the doctors would be horrified. Ernie worked in a *long* store in Princeton, New Jersey, so long according to him that, "You got an hour for lunch, and they measured that from the time you left the counter, not the time you walked out the front door." Surely Hungarian hyperbole, but the customers weren't to his liking either, forever changing their minds in mid-purchase at mid-store. "You'd think they'd walk to the back with you. Not a chance. You'd go get a thirty-nine cent toothpaste and then they'd decide to buy the fifty-nine cent kind."

Fortunately for everyone including Ernie the roadwork was short-lived. A clerk's position opened up closer to home in the central Trenton Business district at the corner of State and Broad, the Rexall Drugstore. It was a shorter store and almost as good as working in front of the footlights, for Ernie turned it into one continuous stand-up comedy act dispensing quips to the customers, French perfume to his numerous girlfriends, and 'squats', contraband cigarettes, to his friend Van Kirk. He either shocked or delighted the patrons with his free-wheeling style and raised more than a few eyebrows when he grew a Van Dyke mustache which only Bolshevicks or Germans wore, as everyone in wartime Trenton knew.

By that time, he's attracted more friends sympathetic to his aspirations on the stage like Sam Jacobs, the Old Chidrull, a Trenton legend in his own right who was in the publishing business and had modest theatrical connections himself. Sam had known Ernie since 14 and had seen the fall of the Contemporary Players.

He encouraged his young friend and once took him to the Bucks County Playhouse in New Hope, Pennsylvania, to meet stars like Wallace Beery who were working there. Sam told Theram Bamburger, "Mr. Bamburger, I want you to meet a future star...some day this guy is going to make it big in the theater." Apparantly Mr. Bamburger was unimpressed with Sam's press agentry, and when it was time to leave, Ernie turned to the assembled luminaries, pointed a youthful finger their way and said, "You'll be sorry."

Sam had also introduced Ernie to cigars at 16 and taught him the master-schnorrer techniques which had permitted him to live moderately well and publish a few newspapers. A few years later Ernie would surpass even Sam in that department to become infamous in town. Along with Van Kirk, Sam was instrumental in helping the young Kovacs weather his postponed adulthood.

Through a judicious set of circumstances and not a little luck, Van managed to arrange an appointment for Ernie to audition for a staff announcer's job at WTTM, Trenton's own local radio station. As it also turned out, none other than Fast Eddie Hatrak, recently returned from Juilliard, was the station's musical director. After a hilarious audition where Ernie butchered a few news bulletins, he was hired for 15 minutes a day which turned into 30, an hour, five, 12, and eventually much later, 24. He started his regular duties as a host of a latenight dj show with a simple format: 20 records in two hours plus commercials, time checks and news. By the time Ernie got the hang of things, all the commercials were pushed off until the last five minutes with the hundred or so remaining minutes devoted to cutting up and ad-libs. He and Hatrak used to read the comics—Ernie mimicked all the voices and Eddie tinkled the ivories. In the Dick Tracy strips Eddie of course played "Eighty-Eight Keys."

The sponsors didn't seem to mind what Ernie did with their commercials, even if he ran them together. They knew the audience was listening, though it was equally possible that he'd make up his own:

Ladies and Gentlemen, Bash's Foundation, manufacturers of Bash's Imported Sheepdip, since lo the beginning of time, are proud to bring to you the radio audience the product of prestige: namely Bash's Imported Sheep Dip. To the Suburbanite, the dweller in Trenton, the man on the farm, the woman on S. State Street, Bash's Imported Sheep Dip has been for generations the important and vital rung in their individual and specific ladders of success. In keeping with their monumental efforts at maintaining good taste, the Bash Foundation will not interupt this program with commercials.

In the ten years Ernie reigned at WTTM from 1941-1950, he worked his way up from announcer to Director of Special Events with his own sound truck and $40 a week, net. He was famous for his stunts with the remote truck: one year he decided to cover Groundhog Day for his listeners. He and his engineer called 20 or 30 agencies before they finally found someone in Pennsylvania who could even find a groundhog hole. They stood in the snow about a half hour waiting for the woodchuck to appear and then gave up in disgust. "Frankly," said Kovacs, "he was lucky because if he had appeared, we were both ready to slug him with the end of the mike."

In 1948, as director of Special Events, Ernie arranged for flying lessons at the local airfield, a wire recorder broadcast the results. The lessons went fairly well until he broadcast his first solo which turned into such a nightmare that he never bothered to return to the wild blue and always seemed to prefer trains after that.

Radio was to Ernie's mind an extension of the ear and he loved the offbeat remote. To get a rabbit's-eye view of hunting season he took to the fields in a reinforced trench, capturing the sound of whizzing bullets. To demonstrate how it feels to be run down by a train (??) Kovacs and crew journeyed to the local Trenton yards. He lay down on the tracks but at the crucial moment lost his nerve—the audience heard the crunch of the microphone and Ernie was billed for a replacement. Once, while covering a major fire and recording five

Strangely Believe It!

PICTURES BY WALLACE WOOD

AT EXACTLY **MIDNIGHT** IN NEW YORK CITY WHEN THE MOON IS FULL, AND THERE ARE NO CLOUDS IN THE SKY WHATSOEVER, IF A MAN WERE TO STAND ON THE **OBSERVATORY TOWER** OF THE **EMPIRE STATE BUILDING** HE'D HAVE GOTTEN THERE BY ILLEGAL ENTRY AS THE TOWER CLOSES AT TEN P.M.

KILROY WAS HERE

THE STRANGEST **SCIENTIFIC PHENOMENON** OF **ALL TIME** WAS RECORDED ON **MAY 18, 1956,** WHEN **ELIZABETH DONAHUE FORSNEY** WAS BORN IN A COMMERCIAL AIRLINER WHILE TRAVELLING OVER GRAND CANYON, COLORADO.

A TELEGRAM WAS IMMEDIATELY DISPATCHED TO ELIZABETH'S MOTHER WHO HAD MISSED THE PLANE IN DENVER.

On April 6, 1897, the 90-ton Barkentine **"MAJORCA"** DISAPPEARED DURING A NORTH ATLANTIC STORM... SEVEN YEARS LATER TO THE DAY, THE RESIDENTS OF THE SEAPORT TOWN OF BATON ROUGE, MASS, SAW A STRANGE SIGHT... THE MAYOR, CLAD IN HIS UNDERWEAR WAS CHASING THE WIFE OF THE LOCAL BUTCHER DOWN THE STREET WITH A CLEAVER.

A **FLOUNDER** DOES **NOT SPAWN CHILDREN**

IT SPAWNS BABY FLOUNDERS

MRS. ARNOLD FRUMKIN of Liver Bile, Ark. **RAISED**

A **CAT, A RAT,** A **RATTLESNAKE,** AND A **RACCOON** AS PETS

Bless our Home

GEORGE "CANVASBACK" JONES a Prizefighter from TOPEKA, KANSAS WAS **KNOCKED DOWN 34 TIMES** DURING **ONE FIGHT** ... AND THE FIGHT WAS **NOT STOPPED!**

George was fighting with his wife at the time.

IN AN APARTMENT ONLY **10 FEET SQUARE!** ... ODDLY ENOUGH, THE ANIMALS GOT ALONG VERY WELL, AND SHARED MRS. FRUMKIN EQUALLY...

31

**Cannibal . . . person who likes to see other people stewed.

minutes of flames, Ernie remarked to his audience that it was getting a little warm where he was standing. Astutely he turned around in time to discover that not only had the flames burned his microphone cord to a crisp but they were now in the process of claiming his shoes. Thinking of nothing more original than "I'm on fire," he hastily beat a smoky retreat.

He was best at the ad-lib and frequently quipped too fast for his listeners or the censors (if they could keep up with him). Sam Jacobs once introduced Ernie to Caspar Balsom, a dwarf who played in the Wizard of Oz. Ernie's intro was, "This is the frigid midget with the rigid digit." Ernie had a natural gift for language and could cannibalize from any language. He called Sam, "The Old Chidrull," which is Italian for cucumber and Sam was Jewish yet! "Go down to Eddie Baker's and get a used car—believe he's not as big a goniff as you think for," a favorite turned phrase.

Ernie was forever talking about *brodskys* on the air..."Get yourself these heavyduty brodskys for home use, guaranteed not to spill, rend or break—double your money back." Few of his listeners ever knew what a brodsky was unless they tripped over one. But if they had they would have known that a brodsky was Kovascian for brassiere. In his skits 'he often used the name Cowznowski as a surname, be it Hyman Cowznowski or Bessie Lou Cowznowski. The Cowznowski legend became a New York "Mad Magazine," corrupted to Cozwnowski. It was the surname of said publication's Melvin, the "What-Me-Worry?" kid. Melvin was named after none other than the distinguished Bernie Cownowski, a Ewing Township local who back in Ernie's day and late into the Fifties did radio commercials in Polish and English and was known as the polka king.

Most endearing of Ernie's Trenton shows was Koffee with Kovacs, an early-morning wakeup program, which featured besides school closings and news (when it was straight) many remotes and more skits. He was already known as one of Trenton's original nightpeople because of the schedule he was keeping and used to interview nightworkers at local factories or dairies—nothing was too bizarre and eventually his listeners thrived on such exotica as moo's.

Neither were studio personnel exempt from Ernie's stunts, especially Tom Durand, the chief engineer. It was normal for Kovacs to practice golf shots in the studio's corridors, sometimes during or after his show. On one particular occasion just to get Durand upset, Ernie painted a ping-pong ball to resemble a golf ball, and cut it in half. Taping it with adhesive to the main studio window, he added a few artistic flash marks with a grease pencil to simulate cracking. As Durand walked into the studio, Ernie quickly raised and swung his nibblick. Durand suffered a mini coronary.

Fun and games aside, WTTM served a variety of uses for Ernie's showbusiness aspirations. As an interviewer for "Talk of the Town," regular afternoon feature, he came into contact with many show personalities who played the Trenton Armory or the various medium-time theaters downtown which were staging areas for Broadway. Conveniently located between the town's two leading hotels, The Stacey-Trent and the Hotel Hildebrecht, Kovacs just had to sit still and the stars would stagger in off the streets. One evening when Sam was up chewing the fat, Paul Whiteman staggered in after a show at the Armory, half drunk and gassy from overindulgence. To ease the agony of the ecstasy, so to speak, he used to take a high colonic enema. He yelled down "Ernie get the enema ready," but for a joke Kovacs and Jacobs substituted for the normal ingredients two bottles of Budweiser, and Whiteman had the thrill of his life. One surmises that there are different connections to be made in showbusiness—Ernie in the Forties on Trenton radio had insight into some of those ways.

The station's location was also convenient for Ernie's own night-life, especially the Hildebrecht's jolly nitery. As a freelance member of the fourth estate, he spent more than a few nights with the boys being on top of everything...man about town? Hardly. At 25, he was still an innocent—he'd been deprived of a normal or indeed stable childhood, the illness had taken more years. The critical faculties which most men had developed by 25 eluded him. He was a generous soul as well as being an innocent; an easy mark, people would line up for blocks for a touch. At 25 he was still nominally living at home with mother (when or if he slept) and desperately wanted to join the ranks of men and marriage. Considering his emotional immaturity, it was not in his best interests to be married though there was no one he respected who would tell him so and no one big enough. Impulsively he courted and married Bette Wilcox, a blackhaired dancer he'd met at a USO show at the Hotel Hildebrecht. They were married August 13, 1945, and moved temporarily in with mother. Now there was one more mouth at home to feed...two in all and only one Ernie.

Simultaneously with the happy event, Sam Jacobs offered Ernie a column on his newest venture. *The Trentonian* a weakly weekly with a shoestring budget. There was no pay involved for writing "Kovacs Unlimited," a series of plugs strung together with connectives but there was always free food. ("Remember Sam was the master of schnorrer and Ernie the apprentice). Sam once sent Ernie out to interview a local diner owner, and Ernie brought along six hungry friends. The owner was flabbergasted, "Ernie, what are you trying to do, bring your whole *misphocah* here?" Typical...and easy. Their master coup was free cigars, they both had awesome habits; Ernie alone consumed between ten and fifteen a day. Sam, to-the-rescue, worked out a deal with the Henry Clay Bark Division of American Tobacco—cigars for printers ink. Each week they repaired to the AMT plant just off South Broad Street near Chestnut in Trenton and looked up a certain Mister Moscowitz. For one little plug in the paper, our boys received 100 cigars a week—gratis. Who would ever think of...paying!!!

Sam's involvement with *The Trentonian terminated in 1946,* when it became a daily published by the Intertype Corporation then affiliated with the International Typographical Union. Kovacs, already a staunch unionman earned $50 extra dollars a week doing the union's broadcast for WTTM, joined the staff as a contributor with "Kovacs," a column which appeared on the funny pages adorned with Ernie's own drawing of a man milking Gertrude the cow from the wrong direction. Not that it made any difference to the readers or "ridders" as they were to be known. To his numerous hats of sodajerker, cigar salesman, radio announcer and public servant *was added the title "ERNIE KOVACS...KOLIMNST...er...COLUMNIST."*

An exponent of Hearstian yellow journalism, *The Trentonian* in its revivified state was a pastiche of sensationalist headlines, gruesome murders, gruesome photos of gruesome murders, housing scandals, tales of corrupt officialdom (for Trenton was the state capitol), plus the comics and the ball scores. Kovacs wrote scrappy proz...prose for the paper daily and managed to catch the eyes of those without ears in the town. A sloppy informal somewhat libelous exercise in quippery, gossip and plugola, "Kovacs" served a variety functions for Ernie's numerous hustles. Paid 25 cents a column inch, he manufactured controversy. He once attacked people signing the Pledge of Allegiance at an Armory show and was deluged with letters all of which he printed. Nothing was sacred:

> Rudy Vallee anyone?
> A very lousy skit on the Rudy Vallee show Tuesday night. Franlastically stinkoo...The Vallee show is a bit weak anyhoo and the audience is just about as sharp as a plate of helf-jellied borscht.

> Margaret Truman's singing debut:
> Well, poor Margaret Truman has run the gamut and when the end of the literary gamut is run, the runner ends at this column. We like to think of oneself as the bottom rung of literature. (Some of our writer-inners have found a new rung below this one but we won't have time to discuss it)...We feel that Miss Stickler (her teacher) and Karl Krueger (conductor of the Detroit Symphony) might have exercised better judgement in barring Miss

Truman to a well-honed public. We cannot help but admire her courage in doing the broadcast.

Perry Como the krooner was regularly defended and just as regularly attacked with italicized comments:

Oh yes, the singers and masters of ceremony from Trenton are rated very low by you (see how nice we are). I myself think they are very good but why Mr. Kovacs do you continually criticize Perry Como (well one reason, he's miserable.)

which eventually drove one irate Como fan to surreptitiously deflate the front tires of the Kovacs limo one morning. A page-one insert photo in the paper subtitled, "Rhapsody in Blew" (whiew!) showed Ernie, pipe in mouth (!!) salvaging some of his ride. Thereafter he managed to steer clear of Como fans...almost:

Well, we finally found something nice to say about Como. Marion Hutton who is replacing Perry on his much needed (by us) vacation is even worse.

So much for showbusiness.

Ernie attacked, lampooned, lanced, shredded, and punctured just about everything which normal Trentonians took for granted in their lives...anything which came into his head when the deadline approached (sometimes too swiftly). Advertising with its hackneyed images of connubial bliss were frequent targets; especially onerous then was the popular Campbell Soup image of the hungry husband with the clever wife:

Buster, that gal is not just clever, she is the local Rasputin. If she can slap a can of soup on the table for dinner, we can take our hot (not to menu) to said babe. Open letter to F.W. (ed note: Bette, the First Wife or Favorite Wife) Cookie if we ever happen to throw open the door with a hungry shout on our moonlike kisser and should a can of zup be open and ready, ditch it someplace and just say you didn't feel like cooking.

When he had enough time to think of something really witty, he invented print characters as altar egos like Aunt Torchy, a crochety old lady who zinged 'em in on smalltown hypocricies:

Aunt Torchy says:
It's easy to spot a phony but they change the rules with each generation and you gotta keep up-to-date with the new rules...This year's phony is the guy who tells everyone he's on the waiting list for a Cadillac convertible...Knows danged well the waiting list is the safest place to be when you can't afford that sooper jaloppie.

Or smart aphorisms for the cosmopolitan observer:

Foo Philosophies No. 268½: a bird in the hand is worth two from the balcony.

and when on, he was brilliant and black humored:
We take a peek into our portable plastic ball at the future. A radio station is going on the air...The red light goes on...The announcer says, "A very good morning ladies and gentlemen...This is WA to Z the Alphabet Soup Network, going on the air. The first hour of broadcasting is sponsored by the Dunka Company...Dunka, the only caffein with coffee completely removed...Remember, if you have doughnuts and coffee, don't hesitate to Dunka. The two hours following the Dunka program are sponsored by Ebony Soap Corporation...Ebony, the all-black soap that conceals your blackheads. Remember to ask for Ebony...It doesn't float, it doesn't do fine things...it's lousy soap, but it looks grand on your sink."

ERNIE KOVACS 47

Ebony the maker of Zud, the soap powder that does everything...cleans teeth, spotwelds, tightens leaky faucets, kills ants, roaches, and lice...The experimental laboratories of Zud are working on a new Zud feature, in fact we may SOON be able to make the announcement that Zud washes clothes!

And now Zud presents, "Texas Dallas." This program seeks the answer to the question on every' woman's lips, "Can a Woman of 33 find Teen-age Romance?" The regular round table forum today will seek an answer to the question of the week, "Do Wife Beaters Make Good Husbands"...And so, Station WA to Z, leaves the air for a complete day of silence...The remaining portion of our broadcast is sponsored by the Eureka Ear Trumpet Company...Remember their slogan, "We can't all be Harry James but we CAN own a Eureka Ear Trumpet."

Between the radio station and the column, there was no element of Ernie's personal life which wasn't public business. If you lived in Trenton during the Forties you lived with Ernie, like that friend never met who was always around. Beside bits of humor, gossip and plugs, Ernie also championed the condition of the city's restaurants, racial equality, pension parity, the plight of convicts—and even rented himself an apartment...or tried:

> We know you have troubles of your own, and we don't want to seem like we're protroodin'....But
>
> DO YOU HAVE AN APARTMENT BUN-GALOW OR HOUSE FOR RENT AND FOR THE F.W. A FUTURE TINY-FEET-PATTER AND US (me)?
>
> We don't want to appear selfish in taking an inch or two of the column for ourselves, but having done it for some of our ridders, we're hoping you'll forgive us once and a while...if we can dig up the downpayment we'll buy the place...signed one very despirate kolimnist.

The spelling in the kollim...(kolum?...skip it)...in the paper appeared a little unorthodox to some, but considering the circumstances of same it was a miracle it went in at all. "Kovacs" came in haste to the typesetters, sometimes days in advance of publication, but always on or near the midnight copy deadline. He was famous around *The Trentonian* cityroom for charging into its small two-by-four offices on Front Street wearing pajamas under his trousers, ringing the bell out front for all it was worth, and screaming like Brett Baxter, star reporter, "STOP THE PRESSES!!!" a sally to which the hardened compositors genially replied with equal good humor "GETTAOUTTAHERE YA BIG MOOSE." It must be said to their credit that they valiantly tried to correct Ernie's spelling when possible, but the "ridders" understood anyway...they had to.

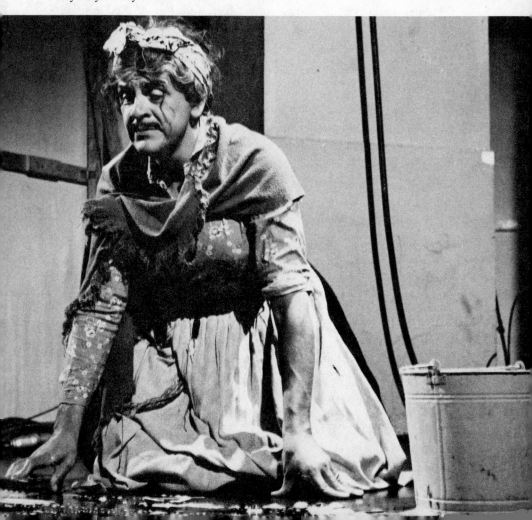

There were other fringe benefits to being Trenton's resident media wizard for *Trentonian* readers. When Ernie took vacations they could read guest dispatches by celebrities like Fibber McGee and Molly, Bob Hope, Jack Carson, Jack Benny, Bing Crosby, and yes, even Perry Como. He brought a certain cosmopolitan flavor to the state's capitol as well as a certain pride, and he combined all those qualities in a stunt to end all stunts at the 1949 State Fair.

Ernie didn't exactly plan to stay up for seven and a half days for the state fair; it happened spontaneously as a result of a quip to the Program Director when he saw his schedule for the week, "I might as well live at the Fair Grounds," said E. Knowing good publicity, Ernie's insomnia, and his crying need for money, the PD proposed that in exchange for the stunt, Ernie would receive an extra two weeks paid-vacation bonus...for sleep, why not? In addition to his regularly scheduled dj show from 12 midnight to 9 AM and his popular "Talk of the Town" from 1-1:30 in the afternoon, Ernie was stationbreak announcer from 9-to-1 and standby announcer from 1:30 to midnight, periodically checking in to assure his audience that he was still awake.

The column was cranked out daily. Perforce though as the lance was tilted toward Morpheus to smash Milton Berle's stated record of 18 hours, the columns became more interspersed with ellipses half-completed sentences. After seven full days of sleeplessness, living in a glass box on the fair grounds, Ernie's fortitude gave out and a few of his friends 'assisted' him in the completion of the stunt. It is still discussed in Trenton.

> How to Change a Baby
> First you must get your materials for one change: (1) a
> baby; (2) a belly band; (3) a nightgown; (4) a shirt; (5) a
> blanket; (6) several diapers; (7) one pair of bloodshot eyes,
> to be inserted in the place of those you normally use.

Ernie's extroverted media personality coupled with the "Our Town" atmosphere of the greater Trenton area made an increasingly impossible affair, and with the schedule he kept, what time did he have? When the children were old enough, Bette, a Daytona Beach native took the girls down south for a vacation leaving Ernie, sometimes for as long as a month and a half, and unhealthy from cigar smoke our old eyes will be tres weaker from 'squeezing em' in trying to make the inside straights." He couldn't move without someone seeing something, or thinking same:

> With the F.W. and two progeny off to Florida for a month or so, we find ourselves the target for the Suspicious Eye. There is a friendly bevy of good folk tres anxious to report to the F.W. by Anonymous Mail when she returns. At the Lambertville Music Circus, a young lady selling gardinias approached us to change a five spot and we saw three notebooks appear in the hands of the standersby.

The strains of the marriage spilled over into the pages of *The Trentonian* when the F.W. mentioned Florida the previous night:

> No New Jerseyite lives that agony we live with the Florida Chamber of Commerce. We firmly believe we have married the Chamber of Commerce. The F.W. comes from Daytona Beach and the most damnable situations have arisen in our three years of martial...er marital bliss. We haven't tasted a Sunkist orange in three years...and the most agonizing experience above all is our futile attempt to convince the F.W. that Florida is having a hurricane when Florida is having a hurricane...She says she lived there 'all her life' and never saw one...We've taken her to newsreels showing tropical palms being whipped around and she says it's nothin but lies. Honestly, we are not kidding...We actually have to go through this every time a storm hits Florida.

ERNIE KOVACS 51

By the late Forties Kovacs was Trenton's most highly visible first citizen—no event, no charity function, or governor's ball was complete without Ernie with or without his microphone. You couldn't miss him if you tried (he'd possibly miss running you down on the streets—a fast driver with quick reflexes). Some remember him stalking down the center-of-town streets wrapped in an opera cloak—mephisto in spats. He was Trenton's Mister Cigar, a visible symbol of town solidarity, though personally he was less than solid for all his easy charm—an uneasy adult in an adult world.

With his entrenched patterns of consumption and his dark Hungarian temperament, being married was not the best solution for his problems. But getting married and moving back into his mother's house was a disastrous mistake. Between Bette and Mary there were always fights over money with Ernie in the middle. He was smart enough to keep working and out of the house. Financial problems compounded his already moody temperament making him alternately sullen and explosive. He was always accusing his wife of cheating on him, but whether she did or not was a moot point in the relationship.

Mary who had exercised a more than unhealthy maternal concern in his welfare was almost as bad as a wife. By 1947, Ernie and Bette moved from over the candystore into what he called in the paper "our ivy-colored rathole" in Mercerville, New Jersey. He tried to play the part of the ardent husband in print though a certain degree of bitchiness crept into his writing:

> Some day when we collect some long, long overdue poker debts (Yoo-Hoo) we would like to invest in those fancy mo-om pitchers. We were torn between a television set and another electrical gadget for the F.W. last Christmas. But we decided on the other one and she tells us she MUCH ruther have a washing machine anyway and she's glad we bought it. She was SO happy in fact, she was crying. Even CUSIN, we recall.

Start calling you wife Cookie in print and the sacarine sentimentality wears thin. Not that the marriage couldn't work, Bette and Ernie couldn't work within marriage. His only happiness was his children: Bette Lee born May 17, 1947, and Kippie born January 5, 1949, and he was devoted to their welfare. Readers were apprized of the happy events in the column and treated to nite dissertations on fatherhood:

As the marriage deteriorated Ernie made every attempt to salvage what little remained, if not for himself, at least for his offspring. He managed to buy a house, and in order to meet the $115 mortgage payments for his 'rathole,' took another job as the emcee for the Thursday night wrestling matches in the Trenton Armory. He thought that wrestling provided a little extra glamour though he was beginning to tire of being Trenton's media cheese (or ham). He was working around the clock to feed his lifestyle—compromising his tastes, the demands of the poker table (with a stream of IOU's), his wife and children's welfare...he was losing.

Despite the numerous demands made on his time, Kovacs still managed to act and teamed up with Bill Walker, a dramatics teacher at Junior Highschool #3 in Trenton (whose father had married Ernie and Bette in 1945). The Prospect Players were in need of a lead for Moliere's *La Malade Imaginaire*—Walker chose Kovacs.

The Prospect Players were a step above the Contemporary Players of yore—no shyster producers with flashy blonds, no debts, just hard work. One week they would do *Hedda Gabbler,* the next *Ernest Slick From Pumpkin Crick,* or *La Malade Imaginaire,* or even the deathless *Ten Nights in a Barroom,* but not thank heavens, *East Lynne.* That would have been curtains.

Bill and Ernie rotated the directorial duties and alternated leads, though Ernie was a case to direct, "You'd go out of your mind because he would get the whole theme of the show, the thread of the thing...but the tagline would never be there so that some of the people less adept then he was at ad-libbing would be left onstage looking like fools while Ernie would pull out his cigar with his grin as though everybody else had forgotten his lines and of course nobody had—it was Ernie." Bill learned finally that either it was Ernie's show or no one's. A few years later when Ernie had his own troop would train them for the ad-lib with directions like "When I flair my upstage nostril...watchout." Theater was a passing amusement Ernie needed an out.

In 1949, his life was shattered when Bette deserted him leaving Ernie with the children and Mary. For a while he was dashing back and forth changing diapers, fixing meals, and generally going crazy hiring baby sitters. He was determined to preserve their home at any cost. He made a temporary truce with his mother and she moved in to take care of the children. As far as his public life, Ernie was merely going through the motions. His friends tried to fix him up, but he was totally disinterested in any woman now.

For the hell of it, he sent a wrestling tape to WPTZ, a small NBC-affiliated TV station in Philadelphia which was looking for a weekend announcer. They'd heard of his fame and accepted him without even listening to the tape. Ernie soon started commuting between Philadelphia and Trenton on weekends while the station figured out how best to use him. A few months afterwards, WPTZ made him host of "Deadline for Dinner" an afternoon cooking show for lazy housewives. He was almost out of the nest now—he had more catching up to do.

Dead Lion for Breakfast

3

e·e·f·m·s
EARLY EYEBALL FRATERNAL AND MARCHING SOCIETY

"3 TO GET READY"

It's been real

EEFM

EEFM-1

WPTZ CHANNEL **3**

Code of E.E.F.M.S. *

1. An EEFM is a male.
   A- or a female.
   B- or an interested in either political party.
2. An EEFM never sleeps later than 8:30.
   A- Unless he or she is deathly ill.
   B- Unless he or she is deathly...er dead, that is.
3. An EEFM makes less than $987,648.23 per anum.
   (Slightly higher in the South and Southwest)
4. An EEFM may not raise ostriches or parsley
   for profit without permission of EEFM-1

*Early Eyeball Fraternal Marching Society

III. Dead Lion for Breakfast

Kovacs officially opened Philadelphia's media eye March 20, 1950, with "Deadline for Dinner," soon nicknamed by Ernie "Dead Lion for Breakfast"...the format was pure corn either way. The host held the spatula while some local culinary celebrity prepared his piece. Too straight not to tamper with, Ernie turned the show's format to his own devices, making the chefs the straightmen. One individual had the chutzpah to create a hamburger for Dead Lion which took a total of five minutes to shape, roll, and cook. What was he going to do? Any fool can cook a hamburger. Ernie asked the smug gastronome what he would suggest serving along *with* the burger.

"Whatever you like," replied the chef.

"Well, for instance...?", Kovacs insisted.

"Everybody likes something different," the man replied. "I wouldn't presume to tell people what to eat with their hamburgers."

"Listen," snarled Kovacs, "it doesn't take any mental giant to make a hamburger. Now what do you do to brighten them up?"

And on and on...for twenty-five minutes, just in time for the next show. An ad-lib by any other name would still smell like eggs Scavok. *Eggs Scavok*?? Yes indeed, a famous Kovacs recipe concocted when no one showed up for the program (Scavok is Kovacs spelled backwards, silly)—a masterpiece so vile that it stunk up the whole set after it boiled over during a commercial. Ernie called it an old family recipe and the technicians were forever wondering after that whose family it was. Eventually the station hired a permanent chef—Albert Mathis from Gulf Mills, an exclusive Main Line country club—to assist him. Mathis turned out to be such a perfect straightman that they eventually did commercials together.

Joe Behar, then 24, was Ernie's Philadelphia director (if you can use that word loosely) for Dead Lion and all his other shows, though he did little more than shove Ernie in front of the camera, cover his eyes and hope for the best. What visual and culinary debauches transpired over the show's two-year-plus run from March 20, to April, 1952, can best be left to the reader's imagination. Behar however did remember the essence, "It was like what they do now when they do sketches about a cooking show and a guy gets loaded or gets funny or makes a mess. That's what Ernie would do with him (Mathis). The guy would try to make a dish and Ernie would just screw it up completely. Not all the time though, he was fair enough to give the guy a break as far as the ingredients"...What Joe meant is that Ernie would get the directions almost right so that any housewife foolish enough to want to prepare a dish would have an approximate idea...approximate but never exact.

Stunned by the success of "Deadline," the management in August placed Ernie on another show called "Pick Your Ideal," which was enthusiastically described in one of the last *Trentonian* columns, for Ernie was still commuting.

> Yesterday (August 24, 1950) we started one of the most interestin' jobs we've ever tried...We have a new TV show which began on Channel 3...called "Pick Your Ideal" and there are FOUR (4!) real, live all female models on the show...Two lusch brunettes Mary Lowell and Peggy Deegen; one scrumptsch blonde Jean Wright and 'blond' Andy Anderson who does the fashion commentating. All we have to do is sit in the middle and smell four different brands of perfume as they collide somewhere in front of us.

....hardly a memorable show and soon mercifully forgotten by everyone except the station management who instead of giving Ernie promotions to better shows, gave him more sleepers to resurrect. In November, 1950, he started "Three to Get Ready", a wake-up show which started at...ugh!...7:30 and haphazardly meandered to 9, Mondays through Fridays. With those hours it didn't make sense to commute...goodbye and a thousand thanks Trenton, New Jersey.

To celebrate his auspicious entry into television for real, Ernie promptly moved himself into the recently vacated bachelor apartment of Joe Behar—and whattaplace, right around the corner from the studios. TTGR had been using a wake-up format, almost visual radio, which provided weather information, news and time checks to groggy Philadelphians. There was a clock in one portion of the screen along with music, information was dispensed via a spindle with flipcards on the front of the desk. Ernie drew cartoons in time to the music though he was never sure what kind of music it would be—at that ungodly hour neither was the musical director. Just for hell of it one day, Ernie put a note on the spindle offering two tickets to a rancid movie in Camden, absolutely the rankest giveaway in the station's history. To his surprise the station was swamped with calls. Kovacs thought...an audience???...an AUDIENCE!! and the format became inevitably Kovacized. Between 35,000 and 60,000 people started tuning in for the morning's fun and proved in the words on one Philadelphia television critic that "either some people are so anxious in its early inception to watch tv that they'll get out of a sound sleep to turn on their receivers, or that the program is really worth watching."

Regular viewers learned to expect anything and everything on "Three to Get Ready"—Polish versions of "Mona Lisa" or Yiddish interpretations of "The Call of the Wild Goose". The cartoons were discontiguous with the music or else the cameras would focus on a wind-up toy synchronized to the music...then it happened. "I don't know exactly *how* it evolved," recalls Behar, "but one day instead of throwing pictures on the spindle, he started fooling around so we kept the camera on him instead and he did some crazy things." Crazy things like later on in the show's run, conducting the 1812 Overture with progressively larger batons: a chair, a stuffed dummy, and when the cannons went off, a pillar. All ad-lib.

After a while the records were replaced by the Tony de Simone Trio: Tony, the station's pianist/organist assisted by two brothers. Ernie integrated them into the show's new format easily. He dressed them in improvised costumes, danced with them, used them to open the show disguised as janitors, etc. It was Tony who developed Ernie's famous theme music originally called "Oriental Blues" by Jack Newton. Tony jacked up the tempo, added bells, sirens, and a rinky-tink piano, and thereafter it became "Ernie's Tune" which opened and closed all his shows in Philadelphia and thereafter.

Absolutely nothing was wasted on TTGR—there was no money to waste because there was no budget. Sound effects were provided courtesy of Bill Hoffman, a master of the studio's sound library who cued Ernie for many improvised numbers. Props were tossed by Andy McKay, the production assistant and Ernie's partner in crime. Whenever there was an empty space, or Ernie had beat one bit to death, Andy would wing something different to him from a huge pile of junk conveniently kept close to the set: a baby carriage, a rag doll, funny glasses, or a stuffed fish that Ernie once 'caught' with the aid of the microphone boom. Once Andy threw out a pair of funny glasses with bulbous nose and buggy eyes attached. Ernie picked up a book of poetry and started reading with a lisp. One can safely conclude that Ernie's most famous fag poet, Percy Dovetonsils, was born in the heat of the moment, or the heat of the heap on TTGR.

The most famous piece of junk was "Gertrude" or "Dirty Gertie," a six-foot stuffed rag doll which a viewer in New Jersey contributed from her attic. Gertrude was seen in various guises and various states of distress being thrown off catwalks, danced with, or stepped on. She literally got the stuffin's knocked out of her as an unpaid extra after a few months of abuse. Ernie sent out a distress call on the show and the lady in question came to the studios one morning and fixed her on the air.

There was very little on "Three to Get Ready" that was normal, even if the format was ostensibly straight and they had to give out with some valid information, news and weather. Poor Norman Brooks, the newsman...poor, poor Norman. Nominally a flat separated Norman from Kovacs though it should have been a five foot cement wall for all the protection he got. Ernie used to climb up on a ladder on the other side of the partition and drip water on

Norman's copy or on his head. The audience knew because they could see the copy involuntarily jerk each time a drop splashed. Also just for kicks, Ernie would adjust the studio clock which for most television newsmen is god, a minute slow or fast. It was conceivable that the poor newsman would unwittingly stretch five minutes of news into eight minutes or squeeze it into three. Whatever happened, Norman dared not look up. His host would also attempt to depants him while on camera, as he was trying to be serious. And though he begged and pleaded with the management to either give him a separate studio or plain transfer him to less hazardous duty, nothing ever came of it...poor guy.

TTGR had no pretensions whatsoever. Things were so casual that it was not uncommon for the camera to catch the host hurrying down Sansom Street to the studios as late as his audiences to their jobs. Since Behar already knew Ernie's route to work, one morning he instructed the crew to aim their camera with zoom lens out the third floor window. "He never realized it the first time," said Joe. "Then we shouted to him from the third floor, and when he saw it, he couldn't believe it. When he came into the studio we picked him up in the elevator." Not only did the camera catch Ernie in the act of being late, it would also follow him to the water cooler, or into the master control room, or even out playing in the traffic.

When Ernie became used to the idea of being 'on camera' continually, he transformed his route into yet another set. One morning when Ernie drove into sight, late as usual, viewers were startled to see him dragging along a huge replica of Nipper, the RCA dog. They were even more startled when he stopped in front of a neighborhood barber shop for a shave and parked the pup by a fire hydrant. Without benefit of sound, Ernie and his players staged many skits on Sansom Street though there were some hidden dangers involved. Once Ernie as Herman Guggenflekker, senatorial candidate, came down the street pulled by a horse-drawn wagon. Stopping to make a speech with the aid of cue cards which could be read by the audience at a five-hundred distance between the studio and the street, he speiled his voters the works: a barrel of whiskey for each citizen, 12 pounds of putty, a plastic A-bomb. One of his constituents jovially heaved a pie at him which unfortunately still contained the heavy metal plate. Mister Guggenflekker was knocked silly and suffered a contusion from that senatorial delusion.

An excavation for a future parking lot by the side of the studio on 1619 Walnut Street was once put to use by Ernie in a nearly dangerous skit. Portraying a Chinaman who'd just tunneled through Peking and wound up in downtown Philadelphia, he slipped while getting out of the hole, plunged into an even deeper fourteen-foot cavity and landed flat on his back in almost a foot of mud...ugh!

Staid Philadelphians were further bent out of shape by Ernie's sight gags...they thought nothing after a while of seeing bananas with zippered skins or apples with plastic worms inside. They didn't blink their eyes when Ernie would pull a glass of water out of all kinds of objects, from tree trunks to doorways. They thrilled to his daring impersonations of Doug Fairbanks Jr. throwing Gertrude or himself off the studio catwalks. They ho-hummed when Ernie imitated warped records or when he pretended that while inside a television set frame he was a picture that needed adjusting. When things were slow, they could always hope for a closeup of his perfectly flexed left nostril...whattaman!

Cheapo props necessitated cheapo camera tricks. By utilizing deceptive staging which disguised the joke, (or indeed confused viewers) there was no end to the visual combinations possible. Like shooting an arrow into the air, 'following' it quickly with fast panning until it rested neatly in an apple on Ernie's head—Wilhelm Tell could do no better. By utilizing an off-camera monkey, Ernie could be an organ grinder and when the camera followed the rope to its logical end, there would be Ernie in monkey suit dancing with the ring attached. Once Kovacs climbed a folding ladder for jest, but as he reached the top, a stagehand nonchalantly appeared and removed same, which left Ernie without any visible means of support except for the unseen rope to which he clung—naturally out of camera range. He once staged an interview with two men in a horse costume, where at its conclusion the two men walked offstage and the camera discovered Kovacs in the back end of the costume. Ernie had merely switched places with the second man while the cameras were focused on the front of the horse.

Some sight gags really confused the home audience. With a pane of glass between himself and the camera, Kovacs once proceeded to gradually paint out the entire picture until with a few deft strokes there was a virtual dissolve to black. He also used this trick to lob eggs or custard pies at them just to make sure they were paying attention.

Ernie's own energy at ad-lib naturally sparked his crews and TTGR produced some unheard of innovations for that 'live' format using a variety of homegrown techniques. The standard camera at the time of the show (or anywhere else on television for that matter) was the RCA Orthicon which was carefully designed to transmit a straight picture of whatever was in front of the lens. By placing a lighted can of sterno just under the lens a blurred effect similar to the fade-outs in movies was possible. Pieces of cardboard placed on the lens achieved a split-screen effect, and when a second camera superimposed another image in the blank space, there were further innovations possible. If the backgrounds were neutral, Ernie could appear to be inside the milkbottle, provided one camera shot the milkbottle and another Ernie. His favorite trick was to 'super' himself with a toy ship in the bottle or appear to be trapped while water was being added. After unsheathing an umbrella which he had prudently brought in the event of such contingencies, he would take out a hammer and smash himself to freedom. The little-used horizontal reversal button on the Orthicon, which reversed the scan of the picture tube, made it possible for mirror images to be produced so that Ernie could stage interviews with himself or even sword fights.

Carl Weger, one of the engineers, developed a home-made

inverter lens through the ingenious use of a soupcan and two mirrors, which refracted and reflected any image to produce 'upsidedown' visuals. It was then possible for the cast to appear to walk across the ceiling or have Ernie stage balancing acts with Gertrude, or even have the levitated magician's subjects (with the aid of black velour rope) do flips. Andy McKay conceived of a skit where Ernie appeared to be vacuuming the ceiling of the studio. The tables and chairs were *nailed* to the ceiling along with a specially built electrical outlet with cord running to a vacuum cleaner with Kovacs on the floor attached. The lens was added and presto!

The show's technicians had a ball with the reversed-polarity switch that worked like a photo negative—especially helpful when Ernie wanted to feign sickness with a bad cigar. Film editing for more inventive skits made it possible for Ernie's most famous Philadelphia stunt in which he played in a baseball game. No ordinary game either, for beside playing all the positions on both teams, Ernie appeared to be most of the spectators as well as the umpire and the hotdog vendor. The film-editing was augmented by 'step-printing' the use of every other frame of film plus the use of doubles. For 1951, this technical achievement was staggering. Ten years later this same technique was used for a potato-chip commercial with Joe E. Brown.

And what of the sponsors? At first they were loath to advertise, justifiably so. According to Roland V. Tooke, then WPTZ's program manager, "The advertisers wouldn't believe that people in anything other than the lunatic fringe wanted to watch tv from 7:30-9." Boy were they wrong. The viewers it appears came in droves. One giveaway received 3,500 responses. A free shamrock offer induced 1,700 others to call in. *Variety* at the time noted that the show's ratings were 4.8 and as high as 7.2, which they deemed "...a remarkable dial-in for that early hour." Soon the advertisers came in droves too. The first week there were no sponsors, the second week two. By the tenth week the number had risen to 24, and by the 16th week the number grew to 57. In the last stages of its run, when the show was on for seven and a half hours a week, there was an average of 50. Poor bastards.

Even with commercial success, Kovacs maintained his attitude in dealing with commercial people, and just as on his early WTTM shows he ran all of them together at the end of the show. No one was immune. A smart producer of barbecued chicken was shocked one morning to see his prizes ripped apart on the air, sauce flying. A bakery that prided itself on the wholesome freshness of its donuts made a fatal mistake one morning when they delivered by mistake (one hopes) some stale produce. Ernie took one bite and BOING! extracted a set of false teeth with the donut attached. Trigger Lund, a stalwart regular snatched it away in a futile attempt to salvage the commercial for the morning, but met with a similar taste sensation. Meanwhile Ernie's voiceover rambled on about "...the look of pleasure as this young man samples the very acme of the confectioner's art." Thereafter the company in question sent a special man over with fresh hot produce—they learned the hard way. Even when the studio advertising executives liked Ernie's commercials, even when they kinescoped them and asked him to repeat his performance, he invariably refused and never gave them any satisfaction.

Meanwhile the critics for their part were a little confused by what they saw at that mind-boggling hour. Merill Panitt of the Philadelphia *Inquirer* managed one morning to get up early and concluded that TTGR "...was only less inhibited than a bunch of three-year olds let loose in a candy store." He conceded though after such harsh critical judgment that "It's kind of a strange show, I'd like to review it some time but who can tell whether it's good or bad so early in the morning." When Ernie read that he made up a banner which he stretched over the set which read, "Read Merill Pannit in the Enquirer'...so much for the 4th estate.

By May 1951, the networks in New York were responding to Kovacs and TTGR's candystore rompings. NBC and CBS enjoyed the people tramping across the ceiling and inquired specifically about the soup-can inverter. Eventually they all managed to build their own, but not as inexpensively, one supposes. For a test, NBC assigned Ernie to his first network program, "It's Time for Ernie," Friday, May 14, through June 29, 1951, at the innocuous timeslot of 3:15-3:30. It wasn't much of a show for Kovacs was used to much more space—he barely had time to flex his nostrils. But to add insult to injury, or capers to comedy, WPTZ gave Ernie another cooking program "Now You're Cooking," which appeared locally once a week from May 15-June 12. More work, more hours, more, more, more...so nu? Consider for a moment that "Dead Lion" still appeared twice a week from 2-2:30 and "It's Time for Ernie" was on five days a week—one hell of a schedule, one hell of a mess.

"We had as many as four shows running in a single day," said Andy McKay, survivor, "which kept us hopping from early morning to late in the evening with precious little time for private living. Luckily two of the shows were of the ad-lib variety—using stock scenery and props, etc...which didn't require much previous preparation. If there was any rehearsal it was minimum—usually for the songs or the instrumental pieces. Skits were winged—we talked through the bits beforehand—and if cue cards were used they usually stated the sequence of the business (exits, entrances, props, cues, etc.). With so many shows going on during the day, spontaneity had to be the keynote."

"Now You're Cooking" folded in June, though in August NBC offered Ernie another show as the summer replacement for "Kuk-Fran and Ollie," a popular children's show which appeared from 7:00-7:30 weekday evenings. "Ernie in Kovacsland" 'twas called. To celebrate his new status, he hired more personnel: one secretary, Angel McGrath, because he 'liked her legs' and one female chanteuse, Edie Adams, because he also liked her legs and because she was cheap talent.

Actually Ernie wasn't the first to notice Eddythe, Joe Behar had seen her as an unsuccessful contestant on the "Arthur Godfrey Talent Scouts." At the time, Edie was a shy retiring nearsighted sensational-looking blond from a good family in Tenafly, New Jersey, who had studied opera at Julliard. But, when she saw what divas looked like and discovered how much they earned, she opted for a theatrical career. Before her fated appearance with Godfrey she'd won the title of Miss U.S. Television which entitled her to a walk-on on the Milton Berle Show. To further enhance her chances in the bigtime and prep for Godfrey, she hired a knowledgeable Broadway coach who lowered her voice a few octaves and told her the secret of success, "Honey, it doesn't matter if you sing off-key or on-key...just move your moth all over your face and look sexy."

????????

She learned Patti Page's inimitable, "Would I Love You, Love You Love You," and looked sexy but lost anyway. Behar was looking for a girl with those qualities...besides she did look terrific in a bathing suit. Originally Ernie wanted a poo-poo-padoop chickie and thought Edie was too small, though after her audition he hired her anyway.

When asked about her repertoire, Edie responded that she'd sing anything he'd like—just mention it—but unfortunately her repertoire was rather limited to a few Patti Page songs and she was nearsighted to boot. So nearsighted that she couldn't read cue cards and was forced to memorize all her songs and music before the rest of the guys showed up in the morning. "My job was supposed to be a singer but what I really did was give Ernie a chance to think of what to do next," said Ms. Adams. When she was finished with a song, she'd throw Ern a prop and be off. If her parents had any illusions about her big break in showbusiness they were mistaken. They were horrified the first time they saw her on the show, teeth blackened, taking a header with a custard pie.

Ernie taught her many tricks as a performer and commedienne despite her infirmity; may be because of her infirmity they became that much closer, "I knew basic things, such as you're a spy and you're mad at 'X' because...and when I walked through a door, this is going to happen. There was never any script per se. You talked until Ernie was ready, and then he'd go for the laugh. We had certain signals. If he moved the upstage nostril, that meant 'stand still, I'm going for a joke.' Being nearsighted, I had to be close to him to see whether the nostril was going or not. So we had bigger signals when I was across the room to stop talking or stop moving because he was going for the laugh."

As for the secretary, Angel McGrath, her duties as Ernie's girl Friday were far from typical and many times enfuriatingly loose. She was responsible for typing and mimeographing the script, or what loosely could be called a script, though actually the script was no more than a page summary of what *might* happen with like "Ko blahs, blahs, blahs two minutes on loose livers," etc. Angel's simple duties were compounded because invariably Ernie would run in 15 minutes before showtime with his notes, or five minutes or not at all...no typing. She was also supposed to take notes on what transpired each day because many times the shows and the scripts were distant cousins. The notes were filed away for handy reference just in case anybody needed evidence.

Who needed evidence? Ernie needed the evidence. Even when using a relay of mechanical roosters beginning at five ahem with an alarm clock, progressing to a buzzer and finally a blaring radio sometimes failed to rouse him. He'd leave the station at four in the morning and come back at seven. "I was a dead duck and I had a migraine for three years straight," he said years later. One morning his boss called him in for a chat:

"I saw your show this morning," said he, "you weren't funny."

"Do you know how many hours I'm on the air each week," expostulated Ernie, "as much as some stars are in a whole season. I have no secretary (before Angel), I run contests. I do my own my own writing. Do you honestly believe there's a human being alive who's not encased in wax in the Smithsonian who can be on thirteen hours a week and still be funny?"

The boss replied with equal aplomb, "I'm afraid you'll have to pick up your program, Kovacs, it sags."

Ernie was 'sagging' moneywise for more now. Added to his basic salary of $125, he was making an additional $25 apiece for the three other half-hour shows and a bonus of $5 per sponsor by the end of his Dead Lion daze. He wasn't going to be a millionaire by any stretch of the imagination at this time. Besides he'd told his readers in Trenton long ago that his taxman had scared him off:

> Whatever happened to the American millionaire? Ain't no incentive to making a bundle these days...Always had a yen to be a millionaire, but Moe Balbresky, tax expert, tells us a man who makes SIX million would have less than a million after taxes. That's really tough...It's simply killed our ambition, that's all, killed our ambition.

He certainly wasn't going to make it through careful money management by spending what he didn't have, even spending what he did have. Champagne taste aside. He ran according-to-type in money department according to Behar, "...whether he had it or he didn't have it, he always liked like he had it. He was always a very big liver whether he was making a thousand a week in Philadelphia or he was making $100,000 out in Hollywood... It's unbelievable the way he spent money, it would just go through him like flour through a sieve." In the early days, Ernie and the boys decided that they all should learn how to play golf, albeit none of them really *liked* the game, they all thought they should learn. Ernie of course joined a country club while the others took to the driving range. A few weeks later Ernie invited them all to the club and after suitably mangling the course during an afternoon of flog (golf spelled backwards) they were treated to a stupendous banquet which Ernie provided...much before he was making the thousand a week.

And he still played cards...STILL??? he never quit. "Oh god did I play cards! Forever," said Joe. "He was such a compulsive player that he'd call to get a fourth at gin rummy at 11 o'clock at night and say, 'You gotta come down and play' and I'd say, 'Ernie, I'm sleeping,' and he'd say, 'Oh no, we gotta have a fourth, we got a terrific game going, we gotta have a fourth guy you know.' '' Ernie was a persistent cuss and Joe would wearily get out of bed and take Ernie's money, for Ernie though enthusiastic was also the world's worst cardplayer and boy was he compulsive...boy-

There used to be a weekly pokergame back in those days at Ernie's house in Behar's former bachelor digs. Once somebody forgot to bring a cardtable and there were seven old hands in the game, none of them knowing what to do.

"I know," said Ernie helpfully, "we'll play on the door."

Which door?

THE FRONT DOOR.

???

So Ernie unscrewed the front door, but there was no place to set it.

"OK," said Ernie, "three of us will sit on the couch and the other three guys will sit on chairs and one guy on either end and we'll sit the door on our laps."

Brilliant.

"Like a goddamn seance," said Behar who then asked our hardened gambler what would happen if nature called.

"Well, we'll work it out, we'll work it out," replied Ern.

Eight grown men, eight mature men, sitting in a drafty apartment with a front door on their laps, "He just couldn't bear it...god forbid the game was going to get delayed for a half hour," said Joe reflecting back. You did it because you loved Ernie that much...his friends, not the networks, certainly not NBC.

No, they had other ideas. They liked "Ernie in Kovacsland," but they didn't like the idea that Ernie virtually ran the whole show and wrote all the material. No, *they* were professionals, Kovacs needed *writers,* and so they hired a few. They write, he re-wrote. The first "Kovacsland" extravaganza followed the script all right...for five minutes, the first five. About the only thing he couldn't screw up in his inimitable manner were the segments of network talent and filmed commercials. The staid *New York Times* remarked in a review of the show, "Kovacs seemed determined to knock the audience dead, even if he had to resort to using a pick axe." When one gets such reviews, they send you back to the bushleagues, Philadelphia in this case. The closing credits for "Ernie in Kovacsland" make that point abundantly clear:

THE ERNIE KOVACS SHOW NEVER DIES, IT JUST FADES OUT AND AWAY FROM THE WPTZ STUDIOS OF PHILADELPHIA...
THIS MESS WAS WRITTEN BY Ernie Kovacs and ollie crawford.
THE MUSIC PLAYED BADLY BY TONY DI SIM-ONE AND HIS TWO SCHOOL COMPANIONS MISDIRECTED BY BEN SQUIRES
ALLEGEDLY PRODUCED BY ERNIE KOVACS
MISS ADAMS CLOTHES BY JOHN WAN-NAMAKER, PHILADELPHIA

Even with Ernie's considerable salary, Philadelphia was still the bushleagues and just to teach him a lesson of sorts, WPTZ tacked another half hour onto TTGR so the hours were 7:00-9:00 instead of 7:30-9:00. So now Ernie was really late in the mornings and Trig, Edie, and Andy were forced to schmooze on the air until Ernie staggered in. Edie used to show up in curlers until the crew purposely sought her out and she had to take refuge behind a church flat.

During the final months of "Three to Get Ready," the EEFMS were formed, the Early Eyeball Fraternal and Marching Society, brothers of the bleary eye, a sadsack club of unfortunates who were early rising working stiffs and Ernie's morning audience. The membership included people of all ages, especially school children. Just for the asking any writer-inner was eligible to receive a handsome membership card with bloodshot eyeball emblazoned signed by eefm-1, Ernie, or eefm-2, Edie, depending on who answered the mail in the morning. EEFMS were a tradition of sorts for a show which defied tradition as was the phrase, "It's Been

Real," the EEFMS password. According to McKay, the peerless propthrower, "It was used as a sort of signature on all our shows. It cropped up everywhere and anywhere—it could appear on the side of a balloon, re-appear on a piano stool on a wall, on someone's bald spot—that sort of thing. You never knew where to find it. All you had to tell the director (was), "It's over there', because Ernie never knew and Edie Adams never knew." "It's Been Real" remained as much a characteristic of Kovacs' work and himself as his everpresent cigar and mustache.

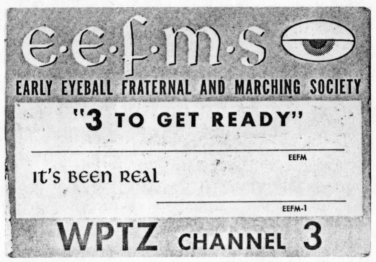

e·e·f·m·s

EARLY EYEBALL FRATERNAL AND MARCHING SOCIETY

"3 TO GET READY"

IT'S BEEN REAL   EEFM

                                                                                    EEFM-1

WPTZ CHANNEL 3

CODE OF THE

e·e·f·m·s

1. An EEFM is a male.
   A—Or a female.
   B—Or interested in either political party.
2. An EEFM never sleeps later than 8:03.
   A—Unless he or she is deathly ill.
   B—Unless he or she is deathly ...er... dead, that is.

C—Unless the EEFM is sleepy.
3. An EEFM makes less than $987,648,001.23 per annum. (Slightly higher in the South & Southwest.)
4. An EEFM may not raise ostriches or parsley for profit without written permission of Eefm-1.

Pass-word —"It's Been Real".

In November, 1951, Ernie was given another chance in the net, sort of a misfire concocted by the big boys which used (perish the thought!) real actors and (!!) real writers. Loosely patterned after Fred Allen's "Allen's Alley" with a timeslot of 11:30-to-noon, "Kovacs on the Korner" took place on the street and featured cute songs and patter danced by Pete the Cop, Alfred a dog, Tondelayo (Marge Greene who was also one of the unfortunate writers), Little Johnny (of Phillip MORISSSSS fame), Ernie (who played himself) and Edie (who they let sing once and a while). Kovacs on the Korner was more than unfortunate; it was dumb beyond belief, and with an introduction like the following, the reader can easily imagine what transpired as the cheerful announcer speils:

KOVACS ON THE KORNER...THE PLACE WHERE THE PHRASE GIVE IT BACK TO THE INDIANS FIRST BEGAN...THE MEMBERS OF OUR NEIGHBORHOOD TRIBE INCLUDE THAT HAPPY IRISH WARRIOR, PETE THE COP...THAT GAL HE'S TALKING TO ISN'T POCAHANTAS BUT EDIE ADAMS THE TRUSH ON THE CORNER. OUR THREE MEN IN WHITE ENGAGED TO SWEEP THE STREETS WORK HARDER AT TRYING TO FIND WAYS TO GET OUT OF WORK, ONE OF THEM IS TO PLAY MUSICAL INSTRUMENTS AND CALL THEM- SELVES THE DAVE APPEL TRIO. THE GUY DREAMING IS CHEDDAR, ERNIE'S CHAUFFER WHO BLAZES MORE TRAILS WITH ERNIE'S CAR THAN AN INDIAN ON THE WARPATH. AND THERE'S LITTLE JOHNNY, LOW MAN ON THE TOTEM POLE, AND FROM THE LOOKS OF THINGS HE'S ALWAYS READY TO BURY THE HACHET IN SOMEBODY ELSE'S HEAD! OVER HERE IS OUR-UGH!-BIG CHIEF OF THE

BLOCK...ERNIE KOVACS...THE WHITE MAN'S
ANSWER TO SITTING BULL.

Needless to add, Ernie cordially loathed this show and everything
connected with it...working on such an insane testicle of a production
merely exacerbated the public end of his life, for his personal
problems were intruding.

Television success in Phillie brought him to the attention of many
more people in the Philadelphia-Camden-Trenton area than even he
knew. Bette returned from obscurity after her desertion to lay claim
to him, his money, and the children. From November, 1951, to
summer, 1952, Ernie was embroiled in a savage divorce/custody
battle so violent that it spilled over into the studios of WPTZ.
Process servers, like Keystone Kops, ran through the sets looking for
Ernie regularly, and one day to avoid them he decided not to show up
for work. His personna was retained by a mysterious figure seated
behind a screen, smoking a cigar. Eventually Ernie gained full
custody of his children and a divorce on November 7, 1952, which
guaranteed Bette visitation rights on Sundays and every two weeks
on the condition that, "...said children be removed from the influence
of Mrs. Mary Kovacs, parental grandmother."

One of the reasons that Ernie's marriage broke up, though
certainly not the main reason, was because of that proud dominant
woman. Ernie married to escape her and though he managed to elude
the F.W., the mother was eternal. She had helped him through
many crises in the past when Bette first left, though if we are to
believe the Old Chidrull, Sam Jacobs, "(Ernie's) biggest aspiration
was to leave Trenton because he couldn't stand his mother." Ernie
used to complain to Sam about his wife and his mother on a regular
basis...bed of swords especially in a small apartment. Mary was an
extremely powerful influence in Ernie's early development, maybe
too strong. Sam's sentiments were echoed by many of Ernie's early
Trenton friends, though it was Sam who said it best, "Mother was

domineering, tyrannical at times—she prevented his early development. Ernie at 27 reached the crest of success he should have reached at 15."

It was also probably true then even if Bette was no longer Ernie's wife, she didn't want Mary to exercise the same influence over the children which she had exercised over their somewhat questionable connubial bliss. Mary remained offstage throughout Ernie's future life...even after his death, though there were other more pressing considerations in early 1952.

On January 14, 1952, "Today" with Dave Garroway premiered on the NBC network from 7-9 weekday mornings, overlapping "Three to Get Ready." Since "Today" was a special NBC project, the network was particularly anxious that all their affiliates preempt their local shows, WPTZ included. After much hemming and hawing and temporalizing, "Three to Get Ready" breathed its last on March 28, 1952, with a tearful farewell which included guest appearances by Ernie's mother and his two children. But even before "Today," Ernie was anxious to leave Philadelphia. The cooking shows were easily transferred to other hosts and "Kovacs on the Korner" was about to be given back to the network indian givers. Dan Gallagher, a CBS producer, offered Ernie his own local New York show with a timeslot of 12:45-1:30, and he regretfully bade his Philadelphia confreres adieu and more gleefully the NBC network geniuses.

In contradistinction to his performance on TTGR, Ernie wrecked on the "Korner" its just desserts. The last skit of the show called for a character played by Miss Greene to be put into a steamer trunk for a few minutes of hi-jinks, but Ernie, clever fellow that he was, instead of shutting Miss Greene in, *nailed* her in notwithstanding her screams. Afterward he proceeded to take a hammer and destroy the set, making sure that no one would dare to resurrect it again.

He tried to take as many of his favorites as possible, but union regulations being strict he only managed to take his actors, Trig,

Edie, Andy and Angel McGrath. He plucked Fast Eddie Hatrak from WTTM as his musical director and was off. The station's personnel were saddened by his departure; the fun was gone. "Everything was just dull routine around here after he left," said Bob Allis, one of the station technicians, "When Kovacs was around, everyone was creative. We were jealous of New York for having him."

Ernie's Philadelphia story was to be repeated again in New York as a one-man production company, but that attitude was special, especially in Philadelphia. "We had latitude to use the tv medium then," said Andy McKay, "something which couldn't happen in today's formula-ridden world of tv. There was a fresh and, above all, adult approach which was inspiring and gave us all a sense of creativeness—of having furthered the medium along its true course, not aping radio or the stage." Rolland Tooke, erstwhile program manager for WPTZ, stated the rest, "The industry no longer offers such an opportunity. It is now a world of time, budgets, ratings, sponsors, pressure groups, and play-it-safe programming. The result of the change is simple: An Ernie Kovacs coming along today wouldn't be allowed in front of a camera."

Kovachior, Kovachior, New York beckoned a second time, and this Ernie Kovacs would not be denied. Never again would he be denied—ten years away from Santa Monica Blvd. and stasis death.

ADMIT ONE
-- 1 --
PASSING STRANGER

Ko with pistol on black velour, shoots plate, first shot
smashed plate...second shot, missed, third (Andy reaches
around black curtain and smashes plate with hammer)...Ko turns to camera...fade to titles

"One CBS executive didn't go out to lunch so they spent
some money on scenery."
note on Kovacs Unlimited script—5/22/52

"Where the hell did you get those," exclaimed Eddie Hatrak after
seeing Ernie's $250 interview —special shoes purchased for CBS.
Not that Ernie didn't trust Gallagher's word, he just wanted to
make sure *THEY* knew this was no Philadelphia schnook they'd
hired.

"This is gonna do it, this is gonna sell me," replied Ernie in extravagant defense. Gallagher delivered the job but precious little else; for that matter Ernie could as easily been sleepwalking through another insomniac episode of "Three to Get Ready," for the stupendous budget he was afforded. Bright lights indeed!—that little pencilled note of June 22, 1952 wasn't Hungarian hyperbole either. If he was expecting the king's treatment for the lion's share of the work he'd done on WPTZ, he was mistaken. CBS assumed they'd hired the local eccentric (with or without the shoes) for the 12:15-1:30 weekly show, and Ernie wasn't about to disappoint THEM. Mid-morning television in New York in the early Fifties was almost as big a video wasteland as Philadelphia early-morning television. Good-o, thought Ernie, those idiots aren't going to watch anyway, *I*'ll just do what *I* want...*they'll see.*

Kovacs Unlimited emanating from CBS studio 60, commencing April 21, 1952, could as well have been a Philadelphia outtake vision. Ernie had a deer's head which hung over his desk; a few flats; some songs—an interview or two, and a skit. What can you do with 45 minutes when your only audience is shut-ins? To anybody else stranded in that time-zone it would have been curtains, but Ernie was used to curtains....black velour curtains if possible. Beside Gertrude who was still having the stuffings knocked out of her, there was that damned deer's head. Sometimes it would be smoking cigarettes, sometimes the cigarettes would be loaded—bang...yuk. No commercials? Try Lost Beer, or Briefie cigarettes, or Foop the hairlotion which comes in a pliar-shaped bottle.

Nothing changed, just the location. The scripts were as loose as before (what little there was) though by this time Trig, Andy, and Edie already knew how to decipher Ernie's directions even when they appeared like this:

Kovacs: witty fellow that he is, regales the assembled crew with his factious...er facetuous...er fatuous...facititieous remarks on butchery.

He will talk about slicing kidneys, beeves, and castrations in capitals aboard..er abroad. (Actually, broads do not enter into this delicate surgury)...

After this hilarious raconteur has killed everyone with laugh stuff, we bring in our Tenefly thrush, Miss Edyythe Adams: who will sing that old loveable tune...

Well, at least here was a song someplace...maybe. On the other it was equally possible for Ernie to wing it entirely with directions like "Kovacs blahs, blahs, blahs," or even "somebody, think of something funny quick 'r' hell to fill in the last ten minutes...I quit." Must have been some game somewhere.

The budget for this extravaganza, if used for personal expenses would probably have taken care of the cigar bill for a day tops. "Eighty-eight Keys" Hatrak had more than a few scoring problems with an 'orchestra,' composed of a piano, a theremin, a cymbalum (Hungarian instrument like a zither), a violin, a male quartet, and two female voices, "...and we were supposed to do an orchestral number every week," said Hatrak, "so I wound up doing a series of solos." Ernie endeared himself to Fast Eddie once by asking for eight minutes of Martian music, whateverinhell that was, thirty minutes before a show. Hatrak soon became an expert copiest as well as composer quickly.

As with "Three to Get Ready," Ernie continued to innovate with television humor. One of his early CBS routines was to take a popular song, show the lyrics, and accompany them with inappropriate visuals as with *The September Song:*

When I was a young man court-
ing the gals I played me a waiting game

Drugstore-wolf whistling at
passing girl- he is zoot suit type
1890 era-they are both old fashioned

If a maid dissuaded me with
tossing curls

girl saying 'no' throwing curls at
man a few feet away (she is
pulling curls off head and throwing them)'

While I plied her with tears in
the place of pearls

Necklace of tears on girl's neck
she says, *"Hey dese poils are
wet!"*

or some part of the daily routine would involve charades with each
member of the cast dressing up as a different word.

In the beginning there were few sponsors, so beside his old
faithfuls, Kovacs thought up some new products to interest his
audience like Pancho Paganini's Pounds Off Pellets:

Are you on the plump side; do bridge tables cringe when you
deal? Madame do you purchase your dresses in the stout males
department? Do you use liner hausers for shoulder straps? Do
your friends jam up in doorways with you? In short, do your
associates call you 'fatty'? Then it's time, it's high time you
latched onto Pancho Paganini's Pounds Off Pellets for that
excess avoirdupois...Here's a printed testamonial or two on the
package from Chunky Hippads, Little Pebble Arkansas:
"Before I started taking Pancho Paganini's Pounds Off
Pellets I used to weigh 487 pounds, after I took my first two
pound box of Paganini's Pellets, I weighed 489.

and more quiz shows. His most famous was a take-off (or down) of

"What's My Line" called "Where Do ya Worka John." Here the contestants never tried to fool the panel who were already stupified from too many years of video sleuthery. Finally the contestant, just to put the panel out of its misery, agreed to anything. Here Kovacs played Mr. Brandy McGruk, bartender, dressed in bar apron, white shirt with black shirt garters, shot glass in pocket:

Hatrak- Who is your favorite singer?

Andy- What are your hobbies, are you an amateur photographer, do you prefer the old type of hobbies to modern ones?

Hatrak- What is your favorite method of transportation?

Edie- Who is your favorite announcer?

Andy- Do you play cards?

Hatrak- Do you see much comedy, are you in favor of TV comedians?

Edie- Where do you eat most of your meals in New York?

Andy- When you die, have you thought about being creamated?

Hatrak- Are you perhaps an artist: are you good with your hands?

Andy- Are you connected with the theater, did you have any partiality toward vaudeville or ballet?

Edie- Oh I know, you're from a baby sitting service....

Kovacs- Shucks, you're right (he leaves)

New Yorkers soon enough became versed in Kovacsian linguistic motifs as had their Philadelphia and Trenton counterparts. His favorite word, SCAVORKOROONIE, appeared in almost as many places as "It's Been Real", and it was almost as popular as his commercials for Lost Beer. The cheapo movie epics continued. unabated as the names of the players stumbled toward new heights of absurdity like these for an anonymous spaghetti western:

MILLING CITIZENS

Gregory Clinkhart
Milton Cavanaugh
Horace Greezy
Beechmont Goldfarb
Bessie Lederkrantz
Nero...Arlington Wesmack
His babe...Hecuba Baldspot
Marcus Parcus...Heatcliff Coldsore
Parcus Marcus...Breathless Gregory La Planchee

Eventually "Kovacs Unlimited" did find sponsors, but they fared little better under Ernie's benevolence. The makers of Flamingo Orange Juice had many occasions to rue the day that Ernie became their champion. On August 22, 1952, they were shattered with this one:

NOTE: THIS WILL TAKE SOME DOING AND WILL NECESSITATE FAST CHANGES...EVERY BLASTED BIT OF PROP AND WHATEVER WILL HAVE TO BE EXACTLY IN PLACE BEFORE WE BEGIN THIS...MAKE POSITIVE SURE THAT EVERYTHING GOES RIGHT THIS TIME...

1:15: Trig and Andy stand in front of Greek set...snow is flying on them from behind set... flying not dribbling...they are clutching at throats...Kovacs comes in on all fours...barking...he has Flamingo can around his neck...they look at him (he is wearing a dog collar) and then examine can...they hold can toward camera and we dolly in like a sonofabitch for c.u. on tight c.u. we go into Flamingo film.

Dunhill cigarettes, another victim, sometimes got an assist from Percy Donetonsils, "Maybe some of my poems sound like a joke, but believe me it's heavenly when you inhale this smoke," though it was hell on the image. In spite of himself, or *because* of itself, "Kovacs Unlimited" was sponsored by Oakite, Nylast, Swansdown Cakes, Dreem, Rybutol (wonder what he did to them), BaBo cleanser, and Alka Selzer—so they were nobody's fools but his.

In a shorter period of time, CBS technicians joined the fun. Russ Gaynor, the soundman, took over Bill Hoffman's function and improved the quality of the show significantly. When Ernie interviewed a blasting expert, he instructed Russ "This guest will talk about blasting and riveting...I suggest you hold back on the blast for the right psychological moment and then scarehell out of him with a super-doozie."

Poor Rivets McGruk.

The soundman was an important part of the show—without him the sight gags were flat.Gaynor's timing made this commercial for El Softo perfect. "Look at this lady who uses El Softo," said Ernie running his large hands over Andy McKay's dope-wigged head to the accompaniment of a slow sandpaper scratch. He picks out a hair, BOING! Bending it to show tensile strength and pulling it out, it sounds like the final snap of a rotten orange crate. When Kovacs casually threw it aside, Gaynor dropped an iron pipe. "Yes, El Softo, look how well-groomed this young lady's hair has become with just one small application."

(C.U. of ingredient label: El Softo has no adulterants. El Softo is brewed from only the finest of raw materials. El Softo contains only medium grade lard; pure creosote; crushed imported mothballs; homogenized catfish oil, diced youghart and generous amounts of spiked kerosene)

No wonder the haired clunked. The bottle for said commercial was actually a milkbottle filled with coke, lumps of putty and pebbles with a rubber-ball stopper with the El Softo logo stenciled atop.

No show was immune, no convention above reproach. He parodied a self-conscious nightclub interview show (precursor to Playboy After Dark) which emanated from the famous Stork Club. At the Crane Club, the genial host interviewed famous personalities who just—happened—to be onhand when the microphones were on and the camera running. Inevitably there was a mouthy sexpot who was just dying to be on camera while the host would find someone he wanted to talk to first...whatever he could, was preferable to being crushed by ironplugs from the camerastruck wenchlet:

AND NOW TO OUR LOVELY MOVIE STAR LORELLI LATOUR...BY THE WAY I SEE SOME FAMOUS PEOPLE HERE AT THE CRANE CLUB. THERE'S DRUSILLA LITMUS, EDITOR OF THAT FAMOUS GOURMET MAGAZINE "ACID MOUTH", AND OVER THERE NEXT TO HERBERT MOSKOVSKY, I SEE STACATTO TRAPEZOID THE INVENTOR OF THE NONE-LASTIC GARTER, WHOSE BOOK "VARICOSE VEINS CAN BE FUN" IS ON THE BOOK OF THE YEAR SELECTIONS...AND THERE IS MR. SKIN-HEAD GLAREPLATE, AFFECTIONATELY KNOWN AS BALDIE AND NATIONALLY RE-KNOWN EXPERT ON GROWING HAIR, HIS BOOK "BANGS ARE A FETISH" IS ALSO A BEST SELLER.

and on and on and on.

There were puppet shows abundant—Cromwell Cranston, semi-private eye and man-about-town and the Kovacs gallery: some of the thousand faces of Percy Dovetonsils; Wolfgang von Sauerbraten, the German disk chockey; and all manner of interviews with the reknowned J. Walter Puppybreath, a schlump who consistently endeavored to sell Tin Pan Alley solid gold tunes to bored panels like "The Cockeyed Cockatoo from Canton was a Gone Gone Goose on Roseshaun."

Oh Little China boy went walking
in the wood
He was hunting for a bird to
make
a sandwich taste good
He walkee all day, and walkee all
noon
He walkee all night by the light
of
the moon...
Then he saw a bird and what
was he
to do
How was he to do it with a
cockeyed
Cockatoo.
He pickee up his rifle, and pullee
trigger likee this
Rifle goee off, but China boy
he miss
Oh the cockeyed cockatoo from
old
Canton was a gone gone goose on
Roseshaun

How was he to know, when he
sat
upon a twig
that China boy stood by with
bullets oh so big
oh he tasted bird like that at
New York's Ruby Foo
He said this cockatoo, I will
show
a thing or two
so once again to shoulder risee up
his
little gun
he pullee trigger fast
no feathers fall but one
the cockeyed cockatoo from Old
Canton
was a gone gone goose on roseshaun
weather
that cockatoo is not much meat
but
plenty of fuzz and feather
he no believe in legend so he
pickee
up his gun
he pullee hard on trigger
and look into the tree
but the cockeyed cockatoo sit
there
smiling down at he
oh, the cockeyed cockatoo from
old Canton was a gone gone
goose

ERNIE KOVACS 89

from Roseshaun
by now Chinese boy is hungry
and pain is in his bones
so he fillee up his rifle with
lots of little stones
he aimee up his rifle and watch
so carefully
to get a shot at cockatoo, smiling
in the tree
He say, I no hittee him, I surely
going to cry
he then pullee trigger
oh the cockeyed cockatoo from
old
Canton was a gone gone goose on
Roseshaun

                    (rifle shot)

        *(man with pillow drops
              feathers on K)*

                    (rifle shot)

                    (rifle shot)

                    (rifle shot)

        *(man drops entire bag of
              feathers on Ko)*

    "Well a good try, J. Walter Puppybreath, but I'm afraid the
panel didn't pass on our song."
    Anything for a laugh...just plain silly stuff.
    The mid-morning show was just too much for the net-

work—forget the audience. Dec. 29, 1952, they shunted him back into his more familiar limbo in the central-stranded timezone of 8:30-9:30 weekdays. Gallagher by this time had given way to a succession of producers like Ned Cramer, Frank Moriarity, and Chuck Hinds. Whether they were any more successful in controlling Kovacs than Joe Behar had been in Philadelphia was debatable. All shows bore the legend, "Written and Directed by Ernie Kovacs."

CBS wasn't entirely shunting Kovacs aside; they decided to put him on Tuesday evenings from 8-9, to see if they could draw off viewers from the leading competition of the day—the Milton Berle Show, commencing December 20, 1952, and billed as 'the shortest hour in television,' Ernie tried to break Berle's rugged hold over Trendix ratings but finally gave up April 4, 1953. Meanwhile the morning show was surviving—Edie Adams was appearing on Broadway in "Wonderful Town," and a succession of female singers attempted to replace her with varying degrees of success.

Whatever visual tricks he'd developed in Phillie were perfected on CBS. The Kovacs-under-Glass number with supers and black velour background was augmented by goldfish swimming placidly around as Ko fought for airspace.

The repeated use of film clips and split-screen prestidigitation produced one masterpiece where Ernie pulled a lever marked "Do Not Touch," and is almost run down by a train (stage left). A few minutes later he came back to the box and lever, "Do not Touch...Honest" and again pulled the lever. *Four* trains converged. The third time he didn't even touch the button, but calmly walked to his assigned spot to wait. Then the inevitable came, he stood sideways and pushed them back....then he walked back to his desk to continue the show.

Providence provided Frank Yasah, a gentleman with Coke bottles for glasses, to assist Ernie with special effects at CBS and throughout his New York career. Frank developed the lustra light, or black light, which Ernie used and re-used with vigor and imagination. After treating a surface with special chemicals sensitive to black light, it was possible for pianist Hatrak's body to disappear leaving his hands to play the cadenzas. Notes would float through the air with Frank's device. Combined with Ernie's ingenuity, it produced a few years later on NBC a chessgame ballet where the dancers—resembling chess pieces, and the board were both treated—sometimes the board would disappear. Sometimes the pieces who'd scramble madly around to find their proper positions...the board even changed color. Sometimes Ernie beat a gimmick to death...well.

Assisting Gaynor and Yasah were actors Trigger Lund and Andy McKay, who'd been Ernie's henchmen in Philadelphia. Both were indispensable members of the Kovacs team, though Andy had a special gift all by himself. He was a past-master in the art of the spiral faint, an expert at comic dying; his flopping around would always be good for a few minutes of shooting time during the course of an ad-lib show. Kovacs once made a backhanded compliment to Andy when he was giving directions for a "normal" bogus commercial for a new soap. Approximately—a housewife is bending over her washtub when her son (Andy) comes in laughing and cutting up. The old lady looks up disgustedly, whips out a revolver and plugs the kid between the eyes as Ernie intones, "Are you out of sorts on washday, maybe it's the soap you're using"...blah, blah, blah. Kovacs in the script cautioned Andy to play it straight ferchrissake, "He dies...one motion...no spiral faints...no clutching...no nothing...just die...as unspectacularly as possible, and he lies still without moving...does not put lily on chest...no request for cremation...just dies...Plain D.I.E., Die." Trig and Andy were responsible together for a weekly pseudo-documentary called the "Year War," like "You Are There..." which featured a few dance numbers interspersed with film clips from the studio's film library.

CBS "early eyeballs" also saw the premier of a Dovetonsils classic. A simpering, deadpan version of "Ode to the Man Who Fell Off the Empire State Building":

I see the guard has left me now...the tourists are looking West I
think those tours are somewhat dull...this solo stuff is best. I'll
climb upon this narrow ledge...'tis not too wide, as the poet
quipt Perhaps I should get off before...Oh darn, now I've gone
and slipped. Dear Me...off I go into outer space...103 floors to
fall to—Let me see...am I correct or is it 102? Never
mind...it's of small concern...I'm falling anyway I hope I clear
the 86th...it seems to be in the way... There, I've missed the
86th...not all do that fall, I think for my first go at this, I've not
done bad at all. Say, that typist on the 79th is waving to me,
that's a bit of luck Well I'm still falling, now let me see, I'm at
the 63rd It's started to rain, it's dampish out here, I'm glad I'm
not a bird I wouldn't care to do this kind of thing, too often over
town, I'm so uncomfie way out here, there's no place to sit
down. Oh there goes 37, I have my office there. I should have
the lamps out, my light bill is a bear. It's rather nice out though
today, I'll take a peek...sakes alive! There George Thomp-
son...awfully nice chap, wonder what he's doing on 25. It's
nicer down here than higher places At least I'm beginning to see
some other faces. Say look at them run, Oh see how they scatter
Guess the rumor's around that I'm likely to splatter.
my, my...how so much fun...mmm...no more martinis for you
today Percy.

But wait...Kovacs Unlimited did provide news as per its format— "The Pathetic News," which captured what most viewers
would have preferred to be forgotten for that hour in the early

Fifties. Billed as the "Eyes, Ears, Throat and Nose of the World," The "Pathetic News" highlighted the surrealist news of the week:

CLYDE BAGLEY NOTED LION TAMER, COMPLETES BOOK
"LION TAMING CAN BE FUN"

Kovacs: IN MIAMI, ILLINOIS LAST WEEK CLYDE BAGLEY, THE FAMOUS LION TAMER HAD FINISHED HIS BOOK INVOLVING A NEW THEORY OF LION TAMING. IN HIS NEW BOOK, MR. BAGLEY ADVOCATES TAMING LIONS WITHOUT THE USE OF GUN, CHAIR OR WHIP. TO QUOTE MR. BAGLEY, "JUST SHOW LION WHO'S BOSS."
AFTER MR. BAGLEY COMPLETED HIS BOOK, HE VOLUNTEERED TO ILLUSTRATE HIS METHOD OF LION TAMING WITHOUT USE OF GUN, CHAIR OR WHIP FOR OUR PATHETIC NEWS CAMERAMEN. AT TWELVE NOON MR. BAGLEY STEPPED INTO THE CAGE AND AT TWELVE FIFTEEN THE PATHETIC CAMERAS WERE TURNED ON THE SCENE

(fairly wide shot of lion)

(RP of interior of lion's cage circus-like if possible Lion is sitting on small stool back of small table. He has a knife and fork in his hand and a plate in front of him. Beside him on the floor are two black shiny lion tamer's boots, lying on top of one another. Lion has napkin tied around his neck. As we take picture, lion puts down knife and fork, takes off napkin, wipes his mouth, picks up large book on cover of which in large lettered artwork, "Lion Taming Can Be Fun" and in smaller letters: "Clyde Bagley"

(on wide shot of lion finishing dinner,
we should hold until he blots mouth.
As he picks up book, we begin to
dolly in to read title showing lion's
head above book.)

visions of strongmen who rupture themselves, or "Brave Little Bessie" Lou Cosnowski is still a patient at John Hopkins, Md. Seven months ago, on Tuesday, little Bessie Lou Cosnowski swallowed one of her father's lighted cigar butts. The doctors have been unsuccessful in removing the butt and/or extinguishing the flame. Poor Little Bessie Lou is seen with smoke coming out of her head.

???

CBS was still unimpressed and what's more heartless, "Kovacs Unlimited"—and the Ernie Kovacs Show died the death...no spiral faints, no lillies on the chest...D.I.E.D.—April 14, 1953. The wake was presided over by regulars old and new: Miklos Molnar, the Hungarian Albert Mathis surrogate, J. Walter Puppybreath, Pierre Ragout ze franch storeeteller, Uncle Gruesome (alluded to...shudder...one too many times), Percy Dovetonsils, and Wolfgang Sauerbraten, dressed in mustache, derby hat, kalabash pipe and black fur jumpercoat. Apparently no one wanted this Broadway Bow—no one except WABD-TV, Channel 5, The Dumont Network. They needed anybody warm because they were barely hanging on in New York as the third commercial station. They craved excitement; god knows Ernie helped.

Kovacs was paired off with another meshugennah, Barry Shear—a streetwise toughtalking lowereastside Jewish hustler, who had scrapped himself from cablepusher to cameraman to staff producer/director—who already had a reputation as a troublemaker. Shear was already on the carpet for refusing to kick back a 20 percent commission for the commercial monies he brought in, and he was receiving memos from the brass to keep his shows within the

ERNIE KOVACS 95

allotted time limits. A fortuitous pairing it was, since Kovacs was Shear's 'punishment'...some punishment! Beside being a cardplayer, Shear had about as much respect for network brass as Kovacs did, and both probably subscribed to Fred Allen's famous dictum that "A vice-president of a network is a man who comes in the morning and finds a molehill on his desk and he has until nightfall to make it into the mountain." Shear responded to Ernie's video craziness and technical expertise with his *own* brand, and he was able to anticipate Ernie's ideas soon enough. They remained friends thereafter: "Ernie was about the only person who I ever met in this whole business who if he asked me to sign over my house for a couple of weeks 'cause he needed it' would get it—the only real person I ever met in my whole life."

The Dumont version of the Ernie Kovacs Show returned to the mid-morning, 11:15-12:15 motif, April 12, 1954, and it *was* low budget: $48 a week for props, three cameras, and whatever could be stolen from the surrounding sets. The only way they could raise money was to plug products blatantly during the show. If you mentioned Saks, you might get a fifty dollar gift certificate—but on the other hand, if you mentioned Tums, you might get stuck with six cases. In fact there were only so many times you could mention Tums without collecting enough mints for many lifetimes of stomach distress...god knows they probably used it all!

More regulars were added at Dumont—Peter Hanley, a gifted young actor and Barbara Lodon, a beautiful blond aspiring actress who was Ernie's pie target. A very important prop she was too, for Ernie believed that it was always funnier for a pretty girl to take a header with a pie than a fat cop. Not only pies, but all sorts of other abuse, involving water and mud. She was once dressed up as the Whiterock Fairy—complete with phony rock and pool. Kovacs came in, leered at the camera as much as to say, "I wonder what this will do," stamped his foot and Barbara was dunked sopping.

New traditions were developed on the spot, or off the street, at Dumont. After seeing "The High and The Mighty," that classic disaster film about passengers stranded on a crippled trans Pacific flight from Hawaii to San Francisco, Ernie conceived of a like-sketch. On impulse he found a bum on the streets, and with a ten dollar bill enticed him to be his guest: "Come into the studio. All I want you to do is lie down and sleep like you were on the street. Don't worry about us," he said.

Ernie neglected to explain anything to Barry, and while speiling in the skit's context about the identities of the fated passengers—the brain surgeon hurrying back to the Coast to perform a delicate lobotomy on his mother's pet canary, or the Senator who was fleeing the islands with his mistress's pet gorilla—Kovacs included, "...and sleeping Schwartz," instructing the camera to pan onstage to our bum sleeping peacefully. As ingenious as that appears, neither the audience nor Shear had the foggiest notion what sleeping Schwartz had to do with the skit. Obviously they hadn't seen the movie, but they laughed anyway...good-o!

Although the idea of using apes had been experimented with before in various Kovacs openings, the infamous Nairobi Trio and Peter Hanley were the apes at the time. That mute ape aggregation premiered at Dumont. Ben Gaiti, erstwhile stage manager who was responsible for cannibalizing backdrops and props from surrounding productions, came across a timing exercise called "Solfeggio". Gaiti turned it over to Shear who thought it had some visual possibilities and eventually Ernie got it...(BOING!) "I had those ape masks lying around in the room, and I was playing a record called "Solfeggio" which somebody had sent me," recalled Ernie, "when that wood block came out in the tune, I immediately had a divine revelation—one of those monkeys is getting a shot in the head! Only I wasn't sure what kind of shot. I played it again and I saw,it: one monkey at the piano, one monkey conducting, one monkey braining.

In fifteen minutes I was set. *Then* came the backbreaker: working out the timing. Frank Yasah, Larry Berthleson—a puppeteer who helped with some shows—and Peter Hanley, were the apes at the time. The Nairobi Trio remained a Kovacs favorite thereafter.

The apes appeared in all guises thereafter at Dumont, and subsequent network operations: as an opening before the theme: an ape at a typewriter is mouthing, "I got my job through the New York Times," or in the course of a bit where Ernie pantomimed seeing a girl and asking the obvious question. After getting two putdowns he sadly asks a passing gorilla. The answer is Yes...

Some parts of the Dumont shows were devoted to a few minutes with Red Schultz (a Red Barber surrogate), sportscaster 'or Vino wine, who besides getting schnockered on the air, used a crew who likewise indulged:

GREETINGS ONCE AGAIN SPORTS FANS, IT'S RED SCHULTZ WITH YOUR NIGHTLY ROUN-DUP OF SPORTS IN...ER-THE SPORTS WORLD OF...ER-SPORTS. YOUR NIGHTLY ROUNDUP OF SPORTS IS BROUGHT TO YOU BY THE MAKERS...THE MAKERS OF VINO WINE. THE ALL-ROUND CALIFORNIA. JUST TAKE A SIP OF VINO ALL-ROUND WINE (HE SIPS) AND YOU'LL SAY, 'SAY THAT'S...ER...WINE.' AND NOW TO OUR SPORTS ROUND-UP, IN ENG-LAND TODAY THE THOMAS ENGLISH MUF-FINERS TROUNCED THE SIR BEECHAM LITTLE PILLERS BY A SCORE OF 9-6. A THRILLING MOMENT WAS REACHED WHEN HILLARY THRILLINGHAM, LITTLE PILLER FULLBACK, DRIBBLED THE BALL PAST ENG-LISH MUFFINER, ALFRED BREECE, FOR A GOAL. LET VINO WINE BRING YOU THAT THRILLING DRIBBLE

(5 second clip of a wrestling match)

SAY FRIENDS, THERE'S NOTHING LIKE GET-
TING DOWN TO A GLASS OF THE ALL-ROUND
WINE, VINO WINE. AFTER A HARD DAY AT
WORK (HE SIPS) ENJOY ITS WONDERFUL BOU-
QUET (HE SIPS) ITS DEEP, ALL-ROUND FLA-
VOR (HE SIPS) AND ITS DRYNESS...(HE SIPS)
VINO WINE IS BLOTTER WINE.

NOW LET'S TAKE A PEEK AT THE ALL-ROUND
WORLD OF BASEBALL. IN YANKEE STADIUM
TODAY IT WAS YOGI BERRA ALL THE WAY.
HOME RUNS, BLAZING LINERS, POP-UPS...IT
WAS THE FINAL INNING THAT YOGI SLID
INTO SECOND BASE FOR A CLOSE DECISION.

(still shot - 5 seconds of two or three racehorses in a photo finish)

(HE SIPS) FRIENDS, I KNOW YOU KNOW WINE
IS ONLY WINE WHEN IT'S JUST...ER
WINE...IT'S HALF BEER (HE SIPS) IT'S NOT
THAT I'M PUSHING VINO WINE BECAUSE I'M
A WINE PUSHER. I DON'T LIKE BIG GUYS WHO
GO AROUND PUSHING LITTLE WINES...
IT'S NOT THE AMERICAN WAY. YOU WANT A
FULL-BODIED WINE LIKE ALL-ROUND VINO
WINE AND VINO WINE IS AN ALL-ROUND
WINE BECAUSE...IT'S MADE FROM (HE SIPS)
ALL-ROUND GRAPES...
LET'S TAKE A LOOK AT THE FINAL SCORES
FOR TODAY'S GAMES:

(5 seconds-still shot, box scores upside down)
(45° angle shot of Kovacs)

Good night for sports roundup brought to you by that great All-round Wine, Weeno Wine...a werry, vonderful vine.

If the camerawork was particularly cluttered or the equipment broke down, it could always be a segment of "Audio Lost", a sketch wherein visuals and sound were discontinuous if not absurd altogether...GOOD-O.

An especial favorite of Dumont viewers and those thereafter, was a takeoff of every latenight merchandise giveaway offer in the universe speiled before, during, or after one of those cheapo movie epics—right at the moment when little Amadeus Trebbleclef runs afoul of the insane Chinese laundrymen who are about to lose their rabid pet mongoose on the streets of Gotham. At that poignant moment, the camera cross-cuts quicker than hell to four commonplace dinner settings, where no two cups or plates match, where the silverware is partially twisted. The camera lovingly tracks around while the announcer saccharinely attests (honest!):

Yes, Lady Flatbush and Roger the Lodger Silverware are bringing to the long patiently waiting (and suffering-ed. note) public the epitome of their combined efforts in the craftsman's world. Yes, the finest of bone china combined with patient skill of the silversmith bring you this fine place setting of Lady Flatbush and Roger the Lodger in resplendant actuality. Were these settings each perfect or perhaps similarly matched, this dinner ensemble and silverware array would cost many hundred's of precious dollars...however because of it's slight imperfections and casual mismatching of pieces, Lady Flatbush and Roger the Lodger are able to bring this five place setting complete at it's special price...yes, Mrs. Jones will poke Mrs. Brown with envy as they partake of your holiday feasts or that most memorable of holidays Christmas Day. And why not, for you are serving Lady Flatbush Dinnerware *with* Roger the Lodger Silverware...surely there is nothing finer either imported or domestic than these two great names in china and silverware...and because of these slight imperfections known only to you (!!) the purchaser, Lady Flatbush and Roger the Lodger bring you this amazing offer-remember were they perfect and perfectly matched, they would cost you many hundreds of dollars...*for only 43 cents*

If that wasn't inducement enough, the first hundred thousand who called in were also eligible for an extra bonus of: a jar of Lost Peanut Butter, a roll of McCafferty's car tape, two corset stays, a pound of window putty, a dozen frankfurters and a slightly imperfect Binkerest tablecloth...come to think of it, those franks sound pretty good.

There are other times that Ernie's innocent parodies backfired. One day he was lampooning "Ding Dong School," a well-known Dumont children's pre-school show. As he blah, blah, blah(ed) the program's hostess, Mrs. Mary Francis, walked onto the set and stood next to Ernie while he was doing her (sic). Complete silence from the crew. He turned around quickly and then broke into a sick expression of a youngster who'd just been caught red-handed with his hand in the cookie jar.

"Ernie," she reprimanded, "you've been a *bad* boy."

Casual you say? Very casual, so casual in fact that the musicians used to talk during the show, disturbing the audience, who'd been enticed into the studio bearing cards which proclaimed mysteriously, "Admit One (1) Passing Stranger." Kovacs fulminated against the affront in inimitable scripted fashion:

Al questions regarding music will be discussed before or after the program. Besides the klatches at the trio's location is distracting to both audience and performer. There were two or three cases of audible tuning up again. This is unbelievable. The long wait preceeding "Manhattan" was as amateurish as "Parent's Night". Regardless of technical difficulties when the trio is cued to play, they will simply have to play even if their instruments have just been stolen. There can be no "if's" when a show is on the air.

There are obvious points regarding the earphones for the trio:
1. they should have been checked preceeding airtime with all other equipment.
2. regardless, once we are on the air, we have to make the best of any situation.

Later on at Dumont, Ernie again made note of the trio's general sloppiness: "Dumont and Kovacs would appreciate it if the trio would remain for the entire show, as the sight of members of the show leaving before the end of the program is not an especially encouraging one to the studio audience." Not that it made any difference to the studio audience what happened with the trio, they expected anything to happen. Ernie had uses for them since they were an integral part of the vision. During one mystery sketch he told his passing strangers they would be on camera when the line "One of you is the murderer" was spoken. At that moment when the camera was on the audience, they were instructed to look at each other questioningly. A spontaneous epiphany of collective insanity, mistakes too.

By this time on Ernie's Dumont run, even the home audience was aware of the casual nature of the show. After a while they couldn't tell the mistakes from the script, almost as if they were built in. If a cameraman came too close, he'd grab him, pull him on camera, and stage an impromptu interview. If someone sneezed a little too loudly Ernie encouraged him to continue so that he could hang a bit around it. There was always someone laughing contagiously even when there was nothing funny going on at all. Frank Keane, the audio man, possessed such a laugh, and he was to keep laughing working for Soupy Sales 10 years later, a comedian who was famous for taking pies with aplomb. Keane supplied the voices of Black Fang and White Tooth Sale's furry companions-toot-toot.

The show proved to be so interesting to the management that they decided to let Ernie compete in the evening against Steve Allen who exercised a television monopoly on "Tonight" at NBC. From January 11-February 25, 1955, The Ernie Kovacs Show was seen Tuesday and Thursday evenings from 10:30-11:00, and from March 1-February 7 the show was extended another half hour from 10:00-11:00. Ernie was more popular than he knew; many of his bits mysteriously wound up on Allen's show in truncated form. "It isn't so bad when they lift complete dialogue patterns, but when they steal ideas..." Fill in the blanks. Ernie was madder than hell. Charlie Clod, Ernie's left-handed son of Charlie Chan was transposed by Allen to Irving Clod, etc...it was so obvious that Allen's material was pirated that Kovacs told him off on the air one evening, "Find your own material ferchrissakes, can't you?"

Of all the bits that Allen pirated, The Question Man, was the most famous and still survives in spirit on Johnny Carson's "Tonight" Show. Originally a parody of Gulf Oil's, "The Answer Man," a radio commercial-cum-public-service type program, Kovacs supplied *answers* to a straightman's impossible *situations* while Allen supplied *questions* to innocuous *answers*. Ernie's Question Man was far blacker than anyone could imagine as with these:

(announcer) Mrs. Morris L. Goodson of Whalen Falls, Nebraska writes: Some months ago my husband attended the international sportsman show in New York. He returned on a Friday night under the impression that he was a lobster. Morris is a kind of a joker and at first I didn't pay much attention, but every Saturday night he has been taking baths in melted butter and before he goes to the office in the morning he has been sprinkling himself with paprika. At first I thought it was a kind of a joke, however, I noticed that when I passed too close to him he snaps his claws at me and has been growing a pair of long antennae. Since last month he no longer sleeps on his side of the

bed, but crawls into a large lobster tank which he has built where I hear his snores every time a bubble pops. What shall I do?

(Ko) I would suggest that you slice him down the middle and put a sprig of parsley on his head.

or questions of more general interest:

(announcer) and now a question from a farmer, Albert Hathaway, from St. Louis Missouri," Dear Mr. Question Man, I know that five cent pieces are largely made of copper and that the so-called lead pencils is really graphite, but can you tell me what goes into chicken wire surrounding chicken houses?

(Ko) Weazels.

as well as true classics of comedy still used:

(announcer) L.U.B. from Lower Lip South Africa writes:
I am writing you from the bottom of a 12 foot pit which we dug early this week to trap a hippopotamus. Unfortunately, two of my companions and I fell into the pit early this morning and discovered to our alarm that during the night an 18 foot python had also fallen into the hole. The python has killed both my companions by crushing them to death. As I am writing this letter, it is completely wrapped around my body. Several of my ribs have cracked under the pressure and I have a blood blister on my big toe. Please advise.

(Ko) I sure hope you will be amused to learn that you have committed a faux pas. It is not the python who kills his victims by crushing it is the boa constrictor...I hope that you and your two dead companions do not think me too overbearing when I say that I may suggest you read up on your reptiles before making any further trips into foreign countries.

(with advice like that, who needs questions?) And of course there were always threats of future Question Man episodes:

Well, that seems to be about all the time we have for Mr. Question Man this morning. Be sure to join us next week when Mr. Question Man will answer such questions as: Does Little Orphan Annie have any eyeballs? Assuming both were in their top form, could Man-of-War beat Jack Dempsey in a fair fight? Between what two bodies of water is the alimentary canal? Who is the tallest of these three, Gary Cooper, Gina Lollobrigida or Mt. Everest?

Whoever questioned which man was unimportant in the Allen-Kovacs feud, which was never fully resolved. The culprits could have been the writers, for Allen and Ernie employed the same writers at different times in their careers, though apparently Allen listened to his and Ernie didn't. It is also equally possible that Ernie was miffed because Steeverino was called to Hollywood to star in "The Benny Goodman Story" before he was. And when the movie proved to be a dud, Ernie temporarily had the last laugh...that guy can't even play the clarinet, snorf. No comedian likes to have his routines modified or adapted, but even if Allen did adapt Ernie's vision, neither he nor anyone else could duplicate its lunatic blackness.

By the mid-Fifties Kovacs had assembled a formidable selection of writers who worked on and off for him and occasionally supplied him with material. Mike Marmer (who also wrote for Allen) was introduced to Ernie back in 1953 and helped him as much as a writer could, or as much as Ernie would let any writer help him at all—which is to say little specifically. Marmer wrote many Uncle Gruesome sketches (that horrid man who told nasty horrid fairy tales for nasty horrid little children), collaborated on Kapusta Kid puppet show and specialized in small bits of informational humor like "Oddities in the News" or "Strangely Believe It's":

No one ever climbed Old Baldy, Old Baldy is a bartender in a saloon in Dallas.

or: Louella R. Fromkin stood on her head for fifteen days, she was only able to do this because she was in a barrel of cement.

or: Fred Bimms shot 36 holes of golf with a remarkable total of only 34 strokes. He did it by lying about his score.

or even: Diogenus, a Greek philosopher, was told by a soothsayer that he would die on a certain day in September. The day came and went and Diogenus, who had died eight months previously had the last laugh.

Marmer also expanded, though Kovacs created, a sketch about a Hollywood columnist, Sidney Skolsky transposed Skodney Silsky who punctuated all his broadcasts with furious teletype clacking a la the late Jimmy Fiddler, but who gave forth with preposterous news all the same:

sound: teletype

And now for the movie boner of the week

sound: teletype

In the recent Hollywood release, "Box Lunch": A remake of "Picnic", a key scene in the picture takes place under under an English walnut tree...remember that, it's an *English* walnut tree

The part of "Desiree" a small town temptress is played to the hilt by Ma Kettle, who plans a picnic with one of her swains, the cruel plantation owner, played to the hilt by Bobby Breen.

Ma Kettle spreads, under the so-called English walnut tree, a checkered tablecloth on which she places fried chicken, potato chips, pickle relish and a Thermos bottle played by Ray Milland. As she finishes the spread an Italian cowpuncher, portrayed by Rosanna Podesta, rides by and says, "We don't allow no picnics under our English walnut tree." Just then Zachary Scott, played by Barbara Stanwyck, leaps from behind the chicken salad where he had been hiding, draws his gun and in a fit of fury sends six slugs into the pickle relish. As Faye Ray rides past on an ostrich, two gypsy girls, played by Art Linkletter and Will Rodgers Jr. do a mad gypsy dance using anchovy pizzas as tambourines. The old gypsy grandmother portrayed touchingly by Jackie Gleason, rides up on Trigger's half brother, Peepsight, and tells her children to go home. "Peepsight" becomes frightened of the thermos bottle, rears suddenly and as he does his head strikes the lower branch of the English walnut tree knocking a Mackintosh apple to the ground. Now here's where the glaring error is committed. If this is an English walnut tree, how come Ma Kettle is not using an English accent...

sound: teletype

Let's watch it, shall we Hollywood?

sound: teletype

And now this is Skodney Silksky saying goodbye for Hollywood, US of A.

Marmer was assisted by Rex Lardiner, a sports columnist for the New Yorker, who wrote copious amounts of material for Ernie much of which wasn't used at all. Ernie valued Lardiner's offbeat humor and his friendship. The "Strangelies" were Rex's concept

---

* There is one huge over-stuffed box of Lardiner's material in the Kovacs archives at the UCLA Special Collections room...an unbelievably prolific man all in all.

which Marmer expanded on, though Rex's real talents lay in making up crazy games. He was a literary sort of writer with a wry sense of the absurd who had a thing about sizes, skits involving three- or four-inch people*

There are a few schools of thought on the subject of Kovacs and his writers: the Barry Shear exposition-after-the-fact school (in characteristic pith), "Let me tell you something about his writers: all the years I worked with him I must say that he probably employed twenty or thirty writers out of which the output of those writers could be stuffed in your left nostril (ed. note: do tell) 'cause Ernie either threw the material away or did his own. All these guys who tell you they wrote for Ernie Kovacs I could probably put the output on two postage stamps." Forthright enough.

The writers themselves maintain that Ernie used them as a take-off point for his own humor—they created, he re-created, or he created, they re-created. Ernie used some of Marmer's bits, even bits that Ernie would become famous for but, "Ernie was really the creative guy. I don't care what anybody else says, Ernie was brilliant, he was brilliant. He was like some guys, not a good editor—anything you wrote for him, anything you wrote for six minutes Ernie would make ten out of it." Marmer, Lardiner, and Deke Hayward were the most prolific of Ernie's writers, though they in no way detract from Ernie's talents in their profession—they were content to help out when needed (especially true when Ernie was also doing WABC morning radio in 1956 where he couldn't humanly write all his own material himself). Like the crews, the writers were content to help out.

By 1955, The Ernie Kovacs Show was being watched not only by Allen's writers but also the NBC management who'd gone through a few significant transformations since Ernie had taken a hammer to the Korner. Pat Weaver, President of NBC and later Chairman of the Board, had built NBC into a powerful network operation. "Today" which pre-empted "Three to Get Ready" was a Weaver concept and the beginning of NBC's network domination over local programming.

During the reign of Weaver, NBC was broadcasting earlier into the day with network shows, commencing at 4 with the Kate Smith Show, then Tex and Jinx (which Kovacs lampooned unmercifully with his version called Beatrice and Albert), followed by Perry Como before the normal evening fare. In April, 1955, Weaver was in the market for a utility comedian and Kovacs was too good not to pass up. Tom Loeb, then National Program Manager raved about Kovacs enough so that Weaver enticed him away from Dumont with a one million dollar exclusive contract. April 7, 1955, Dumont went the way of all kinescopes with a show called "The Ernie Kovacs Rehearsal". This was becoming boring already, but *THEY* were learning finally.

For all its good intentions (and all that money) NBC had no slot immediately for Kovacs so they made him a guest on the "Tonight" show with Allen as host (!!) and then made him the host for a few weeks in late August. Finally he had another show called, what else, "The Ernie Kovacs Show" mornings 10:30-11:00 which ran (as he did) from December 12, 1955 through July 27, 1956. Again Ernie transported his whole crew which included now Edie, Trig Lund, Barbara Lodon, and Frank Yasah the special effects wizzard. Shear for the moment stayed with Dumont as an executive pro-ducer/director though NBC wanted him as well. "I didn't have an agent and NBC offered me $25,000 a year guaranteed - more money than I was seeing at Dumont", said Shear who was sick of Tums and the $175 a week gross. Shear contracted the services of Marty Cummer, Ernie's MCA agent to negotiate, though in typical agent fashion he asked for $35,000 and for that price NBC preferred to let it ride and hired an interum director, Jacques Hein. When Ernie learned about the snafu he stormed into the head of programming contract in hand and said, "No Barry Shear, no Ernie Kovacs" and threatened to rip his contract in pieces.

NBC hired Shear after all. "How many guys would do that today? You could count them on the stumps of an amputee," said Shear in character. Jacques Hein, the interum director, left soon after a skit where Ernie playfully shoved a bucket over his head—the two incidents do not seem to be related.

These inadequately budgeted midmorning extravaganzas con-tinued to innovate. One amusing sketch involved conversations with a tropical fish in which Edie supplied the fishy voiceover in burble ease. Howard, the World's Strongest Ant, was nothing more than a doll's set with Kovacs in the foreground talking, cigar poking slightly into Howard's bedroom. Viewers fell in love with Howard and showered him with all manner of gifts, from mufflers to tiny electric cars that really worked, so strong was their belief in the show. The "Pathetic News" persisted as well as "You Wanted to See It" which unmercifully parodied "You Asked For It", a popular thrill-seeker show sponsored by bloodthirsty and curious peanut butter eaters then on WABC-TV, Channel 7.

"You Wanted to See It" was a series of misdirected failure stunts: the golf pro using his curvaceous blond assistant's head as a tee. The 16th notes sitrr, the club is raised, and THWACK! A look of horror is etched on the pro's face swiftly crosscut to host Kovacs cigared—jeez. Or the legend: The World's Strongest Man: Kovacs explains that this beast is so strong he will attempt to catch a cannonball with his bare hands. The camera focuses on said strongman, quickcuts to the cannon's smoking fuse, and back to Herman's perspiring face—BLOOM goes the cannon. The camera discretely pans over to where the strongman is supposed to be, and finding a man-sized hole or cannon-sized man splinters, fades to Kovacs who looked disgustedly and hurriedly away...Tough luck, Miss Goldfarb, you didn't see it.

The superimproved, rejuvenated, action-packed laff-filled Ernie Kovacs Show was still not the attention-getter Weaver or the rest of the NBC management had envisioned. "Believe it or not," confided Shear, "NBC ran a survey on Ernie. He was like olives and martinis—people either hated him or loved him or couldn't care less. His comedy was way over their heads so that they (NBC) really didn't know what the hell to do with him. They knew they had *something*...The critics were on his side with a couple of coocoos. "You'd expect the olive and the peacock to sip martinis together?"

Ernie supplemented his television exposure with radio by 1956, and was working full-time for WABC at his familiar 6-9 format with small writing assists from Marmer, Lardiner, and Deke Hayward. He maintained his whirlwind pace with the help of his devoted NBC production assistant Shirley Millner, and it's small wonder she stayed with it. "I would meet him in the morning afterwards (the radio show) like 6:30 to get notes where I'd go to the studio to make sure everything was ready before he got there and then we'd have a short rehearsal and we'd go to the show and then we'd have a meeting on the next day's show. Then everybody would leave and we'd start all over again except I would get a call about midnight because he'd be working at home or he'd just finished a poker game and he'd just awakened and got ideas. I'd get into a cab and go through the park to his apartment (300 Central Park West) and we'd work until it was time for him to go to his radio show." Yeow! Again behind the microphone Ernie repeated his Trenton format of featured news, weather, school closings and serials: Dan'l Vigilant, a Davy Crockett figure and Space Commuter. A new WABC EEFM chapter collected members...just like the old days, jeez.

Finally NBC found something worthwhile for Kovacs to do in the summer of 1956. From July 2 to September 10, he was the replacement show for Sid Caesar's Show of Shows. In the half-hour format Ernie squeezed everything together he'd been perfecting since before there was video, since before there was Kovacs on the Korner with Barry Shear as director, Perry Cross, producer, aided by Bill Wandell, Barbara Lodon, Peter Hanley, and Bob Hamilton with his dancers.

For yet another virgin audience there were pies in the face—mostly Barbara's. Dressed as the exquisite Coty girl direct from the pages of Vogue, she slowly turned her head to an admiring camera and a pie. The following week she came up to Ernie in costume and said, "Hi, remember me," and returned the favor. Included in this tv summer stock were more "You wanted to See It's", which featured a blindfolded chess champion who beside not being able to win any games knocks over all the boards; the cannon ball catcher; a few choice Skodney Silksky exposes; Lady Flatbush and Roger the Lodger giveaways, one extremely low-budget shiek spectacular, Leena of the Jungle, and a quiz show called "Whip the Wristwatch" where if the panelists failed to guess answers, they were executed offcamera.

His fans were pleased, the newcomers were mystified especially when Ernie employed the special talents of the late Al "Doubletalk" Kelly, vaudeville performer who was used with infuriating regularity whenever there was a serious piece of plot exposition or whenever there was a commercial...The sponsors weren't too thrilled and complained to Perry Cross, who could do less than nothing but who actually thought it was funny himself. Using Al Kelly to explain plots was not Ernie's idea *per se* but it fit in with the show's character. "Ernie was not unreceptive," said Perry Cross, "if Barry came up with an idea to do a production vehicle with 25 people dancing with top hats, white tie and tails, Ernie would add that they would drop their hats or the stairs would collapse and they'd all fall down and then that would be the time we'd argue. We'd say (mostly Cross: ed. note) we need bounds in the show and Ernie'd say, 'Why? Why can't we also be clever with other elements.'"

Exactly.

His 'other elements' included the openings of the summer show. The viewer found him sitting on a branch, saw in hand, "I don't like the traditional openings for shows," he said while sawing the branch and introducing his guests. As he finished, the branch and tree trunk fell over leaving Ernie genially smiling, saw in hand. That may be formula now but it wasn't then. He received polite notices, though the critics were questioning what he was trying to prove, though he was only trying to prove that he could indeed saw himself off his own limb provided that it was *his own*.

Good work boy wonder!

Late-night passing strangers on "Tonight" soon became accustomed to Ernie's insane black-outs—quick-cutted absurdist visions of insidious intent: Open in a jungle, native beating out message on the drum, cupping hands to ears for an answer he hears a busy signal. Man standing at bus stop notices the demarkation arrow points up. As bus approaches he looks everywhere, then at arrow, then up and climbs out of the screen as bus pulls away. Two men face each other in fencing gear. After smartly saluting and replacing their facemasks, the man on the left whips out a pistol and shoots his opponent...not quite sporting, what?

The most startling series of skits on "Tonight" concerned the adventures of Eugene, a schlamozel dressed in a Norfolk jacket who wore squeaky shoes. He appeared one evening in a ship's dining room with a sickening pitch and in his attempts to eat forces the righteous voyagers to notice the pitching of their own lunches so much so they eventually do...offstage. In another skit, Eugene wandered into a sanctimonious library for lunch with comparable results. His shoes squeaked as he walked, even slowly...even very slowly when they popped. After diligent searching of the stacks he pulled out a copy of Camille. Coughs reverberated as he read and ceased when he shut the volume in bemused fright. Reality continued to amaze him: the chair on which he attempted to sit is carnivorous and even his memory failed. He keeps forgetting a word looked up in a dictionary a few feet away and eventually tears it out to the incredulous stares of the other patrons. Eventually Eugene has the whole place to himself, the patrons having fled in disbelief. Mirroring his own disbelief, Eugene, as the skit ended blinked his eyes in astonishment—his lids reverberated like lead pipes clonking...somedays you just don't win. Eugene's human joy was that he always seemed to be caught in circumstances which were way beyond his control—no doubt Kovacs felt the same way.

By the end of the summer, Kovacs was again showless. The morning exercises terminated July 27—"We couldn't sell it, the ratings were bad," concluded Tom Loeb, Program Director. The brass made Ernie "Tonight's" host, alternating with his old nemesis Steve Allen who'd just been rewarded with a Sunday night comedy hour from 10-11. Only two nights a week, Monday and Tuesday—Allen filled the remaining days. But even two days a week was better than none, and Ernie gave people something more to look at than their big toes sticking out from under the blankets. On November 26, 1956, he even mobilized the Army reserves to kick off the show. The notes of Barry Chotzinoff (boy production assistant) give mute evidence of the chaos that must have ensued:

Long shot of 45th Street looking east from Hudson (theater) loading platform. Four squads (36 men) of riflemen dressed in combat attire are marching toward Broadway. In addition there are two sections (12 men) of light machinegun bearers, two sections (12 men) of 16mm mortars and one (4 men) 75 mm rifle. This is the minimum cast thus far but may be augmented by additional mobile equipment. Heading the 'parade' are two scouts on foot and directly behind them Ernie will appear in a jeep with driver and mounted gun of undetermined caliber. Ernie will be dressed as a Lt. Col. (rank on helmet liner) and completely outfitted with combat equipment. I believe it would be impressive to have some manner of military marching music at this stage of the bit but it will have to be handled either on record or by Leroy as the Army band is union spelled M*O*N*E*Y*. When Ernie draws abreast of the stage entrance, he can command the batallion to halt, confer with his scouts and then have a ball shouting orders to the effect of 'attack'. Just prior to the attack order, the officer in charge of the platoon will order his men to get ready in two columns with rifles at port arms and at Ernie's command, the entire ensemble will advance into the theater and 'capture' it. (The officers and men will have been rehearsed in their roles and final positions in the theater with regard to stage personnel and scenery problems so that no matter what orders Ernie shouts, the operation should advance smoothly, pre-planned.) Once the men have taken up positions and 'captured' the theater, Ernie might order a prisoner brought to him and be delivered, Maureen (Arthur) or Barbara (Lodon) or what have you (whom you have). When Ernie has strutted about, surveyed the situation and determined it well in hand, he can command the troops to assemble and they will fall in ranks upstage. At this point we can introduce the message bearers for a brief account of the Army reserve, its purpose, needs, etc.

A good portion of the defense and security of this country during peacetime is attended to by civilians. They are members of the United States Army Reserve while enjoying civilian status and civilian jobs and devote two hours per week to reserve meetings. The men involved in this exercise are members of the 305th Infantry Regiment, 77th Division, located at 529 West 42nd Street.

Until it is possible to determine whether or not General Sarnoff (head of RCA) will attend this soiree, the guests to be questioned by Ernie are tentatively Col. Higgins and Brig. Gen. Kane. At the conclusion of the interview, network should provide sufficient time to empty the stage.

While Kovacs was hosting the "Tonight" show with bemused airs, the phab-u-lus team of Dean Martin and Jerry Lewis broke up. NBC in its quest for originality and bigger Trendex ratings offered him as part of its own Saturday night Color Carnival an hour-and-a-half prime-time comedy special. Lewis on further consideration took an hour and stuck NBC with the rest. There was no sane comedian in the business who would dare follow the new king of teevee heehee; no one except Kovacs, who when offered the last half hour agreed on the condition that absolutely *no one* from the network was to interfere with his show's content or concept. The network readily assented being so happy to be off the hook they even gave Ernie a real budget. "They suddenly gave us Class A treatment," said Shear savouring the triumph, "we didn't know whatthehell to do with it. They let us in at nine o'clock in the morning with all the cameras, we didn't have to go on until nine at night." A singular occurrence in the Kovacs career.

"We never had so much time," said Barry. "We rehearsed the show and found it was like four o'clock and we were through. There wasn't anything we could do anymore."

Anything?

Whenever there wasn't *anything* to do, Shear and Ernie played

cards...usually. "We decided that if we played cards and the show was a bomb they (the brass) would murder us...'Look at those bums, they quit at three/four in the afternoon and they could have worked on the show," said Barry.

"But then again," temporized Ernie, "suppose if we *did* play cards they'd say, 'Look at those guys---so confident.' "

In the end they sat there and worried...unnecessarily.

Jerry Lewis' fill-in "Eugene", known thereafter as "The Silent Show" premiered January 19, 1957, and was finally the 'something big' he had been waiting for since 1952 and Lost Beer. Shear received the Brussel's World's Fair Award, the Paris Exposition Award and Ernie took away some Emmys. A Kovacs classic first worked on in pieces on "Tonight," "Eugene" used many of Ernie's video tricks with camera angles, filters, and sight/sound dislocations. Set in a staid men's club, Eugene went through all the tummult of the library before sitting down to eat his lunch. Everything he took out of his pail and lay on the table rolled away at a 15⁰ tilt to perspective...olives, milk, apples...everything. Kovacs achieved the effect by not only tilting the entire set 15⁰, but tilting the camera lens in the opposite direction to compensate, though to the audience it appeared that Eugene was trapped in a world which worked contrary to the laws of physics. After all manner of experimentation and mess, he finally deduced that the world is cockeyed. Taking hold of the table and turning it 'right', he threw the musty old tweeds off balance with a creek. Kovacs with "Eugene" had married the fine art of mime together with television technology, producing television's first video comedy classic.

Immediately after the show's conclusion, the studio telephones lit up with greetings from the Coast, Hollywood on the line. Stars, agents, directors called. As fans having been loyally watching Lewis, they were blown away by Eugene.

NOW, thought Ernie.

"Ernie stopped being the olive," observed Shear, "People thought it was the 'in' thing to do to like Ernie Kovacs, and that's when it changed."

Hollywood in general and Columbia Pictures in particular acquired a sudden craving for olives. Harry Cohn at Columbia offered Ernie the second lead in "Operation Madball" with Jack Lemmon along with a four-year big figure contract. Good-o!!

It was some sort of a miracle that Kovacs had any shot at all considering prevalent network attitudes. They'd given Berle, Gobel, Caesar, and even Allen their own prime-time shows because they played it safe, using television as a medium that was basically the extension of radio, Broadway or the borscht belt. "When people around him were doing old vaudeville material—Alan Young or Ed Wynn—they were doing old gags," said Harriet Van Horne, former television critic for the New York *Herald Tribune* (now with the New York *Post*). "Ernie was the first one to see the visual possibilities of television and yet he was the first surrealist in television." The network brass were having a tough enough time with the concept of 'entertainment' much less 'surrealism' if they knew what that was.

Network television was a closed, cautious business enterprise intent on capturing its share of the entertainment dollar. "Everybody knew everybody else because it was an outpost. Nobody wanted you in the movie business, Broadway looked upon you as a bunch of lepers, radio was dead...As the outside we sort of banded together to keep the Indians from tearing us apart," quoth Shear, speaking as a renegade himself. They knew there was something to this olive, but they weren't sure anyone else knew. And since Ernie was shunted to the horse latitudes of morning programming, how could they even know? However, to understand the network's side what else can a heads-up executive do with an innovative but unpredictable personality except stick him in the horse latitudes; as for Ernie he was still the chief of the block whatever time zone.

Even with his tremendous performer's and writer's ego coupled with his compulsions to create he encouraged everyone else associated with him to join in the adventure of creation:

the producer:

> ...instead of making you feel less reactive or less functional his ego rubbed off on you, his excitement, his enthusiasm.

Perry Cross—NBC

the crews:

> I have never seen him in any other position other than complete geniality. If he was talking about something you didn't understand, he'd stop to make sure he explained it—he was always open to advice. He tried to get you involved no matter what job you had and looked on the lowliest assistant the same way.

Artie Forrest, former cameraman—Dumont

> *Anybody* would do anything for *Ernie*. I was part of the show, I loved the show...everybody loved him. During the course of the day he would talk to the custodian, the janitor, the program director—nobody was too big or too small for him.

Ben Gaiti, stage manager—Dumont
(nicknamed Abu Ben Gaiti by Ernie)

the assistant:

> That was my life and I never minded it, never resented it, didn't feel I was being taken, didn't feel put upon. It was just the way of life when you worked with Ernie. You still had fun, you still had another life, but your other life had to be from 2-3 in the afternoon 'cause the rest of your life was with him.

Shirley Milner, production
assistant—NBC

Ernie's off-camera life (if indeed there was such a thing) from 1952-1957 was equally open-ended and troubled more often than not with many, many inner problems..."he was dedamned," noted Marty Cummer his New York MCA agent.

In 1952, Miklos Molnar, Philadelphia gourmet chef was still to meet Matzoh Hepplewhite, Broadway Bow and Man-About-Town in his crazy shoes a divorce casualty with two children and dependent mother...

Dissolve to...

MIKLOS MOLNAR

MEETS

MOTZAH HEPPLEWHITE

IN THE

BIG APPLE

...the thing that was always striking to me about Ernie was that he was the only man I ever saw that dressed only in black and white and looked loud. He used to wear a black suit, he had a jet black mustache, white shirt, black tie, diamond stickpin, diamond everything. It was always black and white and someway or another it looked a little flashy. Not to be deprecating...he had a very *outstanding* look in black and white.

Mike Marmer, Kovacs writer, mid-50's

...he lived not only tv but the whole media, the whole world was just like one big apple in front of a boy that was hungry.

Ken McCormick, editor of *Zoomar*
for Doubleday

V. Miklos Molnar Meets Moztah Hepplewhite in the Big Apple

Wifeless though mothered, Ernie Kovacs set up headquarters in a modest house in New City, New Jersey, an hour's drive up the Palisades from New York City where he ensconced his mother and sometimes his children. Somehow he managed to pay her expenses though he himself was making a little more than a hundred dollars a week. Because of his long hours, he gave Mary a German Shepherd for company, though eventually she started complaining that the dog wasn't eating right— "dog's gotta eat steaks"—one wonders what Ernie ate then. She augmented her cheerful messages with postcards...open postcards which arrived regularly at CBS studio 60: "Dear Son: I am starving, please send me money." Ed Hatrak, then a close friend observed, "I don't know what she did with it, but it was always not enough money."

This form of maternal harassment drove Ernie to seek some novel forms of relief to which Hatrak was an unwilling mediator. Once he received a frantic call from Mary in New City, "What am I going to do with Ernie," she wailed, "he's sitting out in front of the house on a pile of snow in his shorts—he won't come in. We just had an argument and he's mad at me, what should I do?"

"She was fond of him and loved him," said Hatrak, "but boy! did she do some things which made him unhappy." Ernie belonged in New York City anyway and eventually found his home away from home...Sardi's, just off Shubert Alley, in the heart of the theatrical district.

To educate his viewers in the culinary arts, Ernie asked Vincent one morning to prepare a house specialty, Caesar salad whose ingredients included anchovies and coddled eggs. Once into the preparation Ernie became nauseous, this being 8:30 in the morning, and repeatedly pleaded with Vincent to forget about the salad. When Vincent was about to add sherry as the crowning touch, Ernie again pleaded for the sake of his health, "Stop it, never mind, forget it, let's just drink the sherry and call it a day." They did—the viewers could go to the restaurant if they were that interested.

Beside Sardi's, Ernie was working on another home...with Edie Adams. Even before New York she was more than just a nearsighted female vocalist with a good set of legs though Ernie at their first meeting was oblivious to her charms. His only concerns were his family, the girls, and his work. Nontheless there was this pretty girl, "I tried to ignore Edie Adams," he said later on (foolish man), "but she was unfailingly pleasant and nice to look at. No one could give a girl like that the cold shoulder. I kept telling myself that I was no judge of women. I couldn't believe that a beautiful talented girl like Edie really found me attractive."

The lady in question was intimidated and fascinated by her new employer. Her mother never told her what to do about tall swashbuckling divorced Hungarians who smoked big black cigars and had two children. What's a poor girl to do? Check it out, obviously.

A few days after their initial meeting he asked her out to dinner.

"I'm going out to eat...Are you going out to eat?"

Tender.

Edie immediately accepted—what red-blooded American daughter of a real-estate broker wouldn't. On their second date, Ernie showed up in a Jaguar for which he'd hocked his entire life savings. Why?

Sardi's was the perfect home, even if he couldn't afford it all the time. Owner/manager Vincent Sardi, Jr. knew Ernie strictly as a client until the subject of sportscars came up. Vincent has a Jaguar and Ernie not to be outdone acquired an Allard, a highly sophistocated righthand drive machine. The righthand drive made it easy for Ernie to cruise the back roads of Vermont scooping up roadside bouquets, but as a whole it left much to be desired. Once when driving up the Westside Highway upstate Ernie saw a wheel rolling ahead of him which bumped into the guardrail, flew up into the air, and landed in the streets below. Ernie thought that was pretty interesting as a visual until he realized that it was *his* wheel. It transpired that when the Allard was assembled in the States, the manufacturers had put the knock-on hubcaps the wrong way so that instead of the wheels automatically tightening they loosened. After that foray into status, Ernie contented himself with a less exotic though more conventional means of transportation, a white Lincoln convertible with two phones in the back (in case one line was busy) and decorated with raccoon tails over the tail-lights because he didn't want to be conspicuous.

Besides Vincent Sardi, Ernie made friends with Martyn, the wine steward. Just for fun Ernie made him not only taste his wine but drink glass after glass to be certain. Fine for Martyn except that Ernie used to come in three or four times a night and the cumulative effects of the grape added up to Martyn being 'sozzled' by the evening's close. On Saturday night Ernie rewarded his friend with a cigar for his Sunday's day off.

When Ernie assumed his duties at Dumont, Vincent and Martyn were worked into the show—and Vincent was the perennial last-minute replacement guest. For one show Ernie asked him to bring in everything from the lost and found. "Among other things, I found my own hat," said Vincent, "and I didn't wear hats except when it rained." Someone obviously from the horsey set left a huge hypo in the checkroom—Ernie was going to put *that* on but changed his mind. Martyn once came on to explain to viewers the difference between a split and a magnum of champagne. After much cajoling Ernie induced him to taste a little and by show's end, Martyn was 'sozzled' again, as if he'd never left Sardi's.

"Oh, I don't like taxis," he replied.

Ernie was in love alright though Edie needed to make sure, just like her mother taught her. In February, 1953, Edie left the CBS morning show for Broadway to play Eileen in "Wonderful Town," starring Roz Russell and while she was on the road Ernie played stage-door Johnny in Washington, Philadelphia, and Boston on the weekends. Was he ever persistent! Finally they had a quarrel and Edie decided to flee to Europe by boat.

"Go ahead, go to Europe," he bellowed, "Go to Afganistan or Hightstown, New Jersey, if you like. Who cares!"

He did.

Ernie showed up at the dock loaded down with presents for the lover's reconciliation, which melted Edie's reserve some, though she was still determined to take some time off before giving him the answer...six weeks at least. Her reserve melted even faster than she believed. Edie spent three days exactly, three miserable days, talking long distance to Ernie in New York. A few weeks later while Edie was in Dallas, Ernie snatched her up and sneaked over the border. They were married in Mexico September 12, 1954. On their return the happy couple moved into a tidy five-room apartment on fashionable Sutton Place, 55 East End Avenue, where their lives were almost complete.

Almost...

A year and a half earlier on Sunday, July 19, 1953, as per his settlement with his estranged wife, Ernie gave over his children to Bette for a pre-arranged week-end visit. When Ernie's uncle came by the following Monday to pick the girls up, not only had they vanished but so had Bette, her mother and her mother's husband. A complaint was sworn out in Trenton Police Court, and a day later acting on an anonymous tip, two Trenton detectives as well as members of the Newark Police Department attempted to arrest Sidney Shotwell (Bette's stepfather) in connection with the alleged crime. After a wild chase through the rain-slick Newark sidestreets in which one of the Trenton detectives, Fred Hutchinson, was almost run down by the fleeing Shotwell. By December 8, 1953, the police complaint became a grand jury indictment for kidnapping—though by that time Bette, her parents, and Ernie's children were safely in Florida. A month later the Florida police arrested the Shotwells and held them on bail of ten thousand dollars apiece, pending their extradition to New Jersey. But at the last moment after a meeting between the Shotwell's counsel State Senator Wayne Rippley, the Governor, Assistant Governor, and State Prosecutor, the extradition writ was voided because of interstate jurisdictional difficulties. The net result was that not only were the Shotwells free, but that there was no legal way for Ernie to get his children back short of kidnapping them himself.

The following year and a half was a brutal trial for Ernie, Edie, and anyone close to the family. Each weekend thereafter Ernie, in the company of his father, combed the Florida bayous without success. No expense was spared, though the private detectives he hired were of little use and more than once caused him further anguish. One investigator told him that he had at long last located his children and that they would be returned to him at 12 o'clock on a certain day. To celebrate the joyous reunion he rang up department stores and ordered tons of gifts. However when the great day arrived the investigator informed Ernie that he had made a mistake. "It was a mistake," he told his mother, "do something with these toys."

Ernie never gave up hope. For two succeeding Christmases he bought the girls presents in anticipation of their homecoming and regretfully put them in the closet. He was so wrought up, according to his friend Vincent Sardi, that he developed severe colitis, and many times while he was doing a show he would be sitting in a pool of blood and had to wear kotexes to staunch the flow.

After almost three years his searches paid off, for in June, 1955, he discovered the girls living in a shack behind a restaurant where Bette was a waitress. At first the children were afraid because the mother had told them all sorts of scare stories, but when they finally got into the car, Kippie asked Ernie whether he still smoked cigars. Ernie replied in return whether she still sucked her thumb and everything was fine after that. At the time of Ernie's death there was still a warrant out in Florida for his arrest in connection with the 'crime.'

Edie assumed the dubious title of stepmother though she was really better than any stepmother could have been. Ernie, Edie, and the children moved from East End Avenue into a spectacular 17-room duplex at 300 Central Park West. For a month they had no visitors while they taught the girls how to lead civilized lives—for the natural mother had done little in the way of showing them how to use utensils or even how to brush their teeth. After the month, Edie enrolled the girls in Miss Hewett's School where they learned singing, dancing and rudimentary academics, though the harrowing scars of their captivity remained for a period thereafter. When the girls went for drives in the country, everytime a police car would go by they would involuntarily sink to the floor, thinking the police would return them to Florida.

There was nothing Ernie wouldn't do for his girls to give them a sense of wonder. He once took them to see Peter Pan and after the show, one of the girls said, "Teach us to fly Papa." Ernie took them to the pool at the New York Athletic Club for a dip. "This is very much like flying except you're doing it in water," he told them. "The children were delighted with that consideration so they flew and enjoyed swimming as they never had before. That was a profound kind of statement," mused Marc Connelly, author of *Green Pastures,* poker player, and Kovacs family intimate.

The kidnapping had significantly altered Ernie's lifestyle—for the duration of the search he had given up his most beloved activity, the weekend poker game. Of course he played during the week—boy did he play, especially with the crews. "I honestly believe he would purposely lose money to us," said 'Abu' Ben Gaiti," he was that kind of man. Our stakes were not very high, maybe they might have been as high as a dollar, but he never had a good hole card, so when you never had a good hole card, you can't help yourself, you must lose." Even if he had something there was no guarantee he'd win. Once, during one of the Dumont games, Ernie and Barry came to a showdown with many dollars in the pot.

"Whatdoyougot?" Ernie asked Barry.

"Fives."

"Good," said Ernie who only had a pair of deuces.

"That's the kind of game he played," remembered Artie Forrest, "he'd think nothing of spending hundreds of dollars on a pair of deuces just to see whether he could work it all the way through, and nine times out of ten...he did." Maybe with the crews, but not with Barry Shear.

When his writers were foolish enough to play to pick up some spare change, they learned the hard way. In spite of the fact that Mike Marmer, who'd been brought up playing cards as a kid, dubbed him "a godawful pokerplayer," he fared no better. The first day Mike showed up for work, he found Ernie playing poker with Barry Shear and Bill Wendell, an announcer used on his NBC shows. The game was pot limit—"I played pot limit where pot limit was normal," said Marmer, "but I remember Ernie just slapped a pile of bills on the table in the first pot and just bet me right out of the game and I had no place to go."

Ernie liked to carry huge amounts of cash with him at all times anyway—what's so awful about playing an outside every now and then, pulling for the inside straight? "Ernie played a lot of inside straights and he didn't hit them that often but he would beat you to death with money...I played with him a few times," said the writer, "but I realized that it was a futile game whether I played cards or not. I never had enough money to play cards with Bill and Barry and Ernie."

Sometimes the games weren't only futile—they could be dangerous. The Hudson Theater where Ernie did the "Tonight" show was an old theater with a three-story lighting loft. As per usual, Shear, Ernie, and Wendell were hunched over an orange crate squeezing the inside straights during a pre-show game when an electrician accidentally dropped a taped set of electricians pliers over the side. The four pounds plus of steaming metal hit the floor about three feet from our boys. Everyone else was a little shell-shocked except Ernie, who nonchalantly looked over and said, "OK whose deal?"—as if it were normal to play in the midst of falling objects in Kovacsland.

Poker was an accepted part of Ernie's working day at NBC, and Shirley along with her other duties was the logician of the game, "The only ones I really knew about were the ones that took place after our production meetings at about 12:30. He would call and say, 'Call a meeting for the executive room on the 24th floor at 1 o'clock and order sandwiches.'" And Shirl knew who to call: Marc Connelly, Dave Garroway, and inevitably Barry Shear. Actually gambling in any form was a passion, just for the hell of it he devised a method of playing Monopoly with real money, and when he played tennis (infrequently) just to spice up the game he'd bet on each point...good clean fun?

"He didn't lose as much at poker as he did at gin," laconically adds Marty Cummer, Ernie's New York agent. Cummer used to feel badly when they played cards all night...and Ernie lost so much...the breaks.

Poker was recreation; he loved the healthy atmosphere of smoke-filled rooms, the frantic see ya's, call ya's and raise ya's were music to his ears—none could dislodge him from that pasttime. Gambling was one of the excuses he used for never flying anywhere. To Ernie's mind there was nothing quite like a leisurely cross-country trainride where you had nothing to do except look at the scenery between hands of gin.

Nothing stood in his way of a game. Once Joe Behar, his erstwhile Philie director, then working for "Wide, Wide, World" got a call from Ernie for a Monday night session while his wife was out of town and he was babysitting.

"I can't come today," said Joe, "'cause I'm watching the kid."

"You gotta come, we need you," pleaded Ernie.

Can't do it.

"Bring the baby," said Ernie, "we gotta lotta room, he can sleep." Casino Kovacs 17 rooms of continuous action nightly.

No.

"You gotta bring him," repeated the cigar persuasively. He needed a minimum of six players and was having trouble finding many since his games were getting bigger. Behar reluctantly took his three-year-old son into New York and up to the game, ensconcing him on the terrace since it was a hot night.

The next day when Joe stumbled home with son his wife was puzzled, "He's covered with mosquito bites, how did he get mosquito bites?" and Joe was too embarrassed.

"But those games," said Behar, "were more important than anything, anything we ever did—god forbid anybody doesn't come to the poker game."

Even without poker Ernie achieved a notoriety which transcended the highly formalized New York scene, and although his morning shows were never widely acclaimed he always managed to have his more 'famous' show business and literary friends in for a chat. Marc Connelly filled in when Ernie took off for his honeymoon; during a take off of "This Is Your Life," Sam Levenson was the featured guest with cameo appearances provided by Morey Amsterdam and Vincent Sardi, Jr.

Just being with Ernie was a tonic. Once at Sardi's (naturally), Joe Behar, Ernie and Sidney Chaplin (who Ernie idolized) were having lunch one Wednesday. At the next table were seated a gaggle of matinee gold-star grandmas sampling the ambiance of the famous eatery. When Kovacs and company walked in the ladies were visibly agitated and kept nudging each other, "Isn't that Ernie Kovacs?" they seemed to say—(they didn't know Chaplin). Finally the ladies mustered up their courage and leaning over to Chaplin inquired,

"Isn't that Kovacs?"

"Yes," he replied.

"What's he doing here?"

"Shooting a movie," said Sidney sensing a joke afoot.

Now they were really interested...what movie pray tell was the distinguished comedian shooting in Sardi's?

"Oh," said Chaplin matter-of-factly, "Andy Hardy Fucks the Dwarf" which devastated the biddies and made their afternoon.

After the children came back to stay, Sardi's was less a home for he turned his cavernous Central Park West residence into a combination office, antique emporium, cigar store (complete with built-in humidor), and shoe store for Edie's 350-plus pair of shoes. A surrealist in other matters already, when friends would come over to the house they would run the risk of getting lanced by the amount of antique armory, swords, and suits of armor collected therein. Starting innocently enough when Edie bought her husband a set of dueling pistols, the collection grew to titanic proportions—not that he knew a damn thing about real quality armory, he just liked to have it around the house. Bill Wendell on his way through the house to the poker table almost ran over a suit of newly purchased armor.

"How do you like it,?" Ernie genially inquired.

"Very impressive," said Wendell.

"I just bought it all for $750."

"Why?"

"Very good buy," said Ernie.

Money was only money to Kovacs, needless to say—it was all one big kick—even when he couldn't really spend it, he spent it...why not, he earned it. During the period when his daughters were kidnapped he was in hock to private detectives for $50,000—any sane man in such a financial bind would have tried to economize, but not Ernie. As much a part of his rituals as poker with the boys, was lunch at Sardi's...his treat, be it Shear or anybody else who stayed around for lunch...the fastest tab in the East. He was adamant about it, "...Ernie would never let me pick up the check," said Shear, "He was impossible because he would get angry, really angry as opposed to fake angry." Shear finally managed to broach the subject over lunch.

"Ernie, we know each other pretty well," temporized Shear, "we've been working together five or six days a week for almost a year...whathehell are you eating in Sardi's for if you're in hock up to your ass."

"The answer is very simple," Ernie replied evenly, "I owe the man seven thousand dollars and if I don't continue showing up he's going to ask for the money."

Now there's a basic logic at work here, wasn't there?

With reasoning like that, anything's possible. Once the children were rescued, the apartment on Central Park West was the center of his life. He couldn't be pried out of there, always being at work after the children were in bed. "No matter when I walked into Ernie's apartment, two, three, four, five o'clock in the morning with my material he was always awake," said Mike Marmer. "I don't know when the hell Ernie ever slept. There was some talk he got two hours worth a night." Well, more between two hours and 45 minutes according to Ernie himself, depending on whether the cards or the typewriter were running. When pressed on the subject of sleep, Ernie replied that he really didn't get by exactly, "I feel lousy all the time." The onerous schedule he'd set for himself in 1956—the NBC show, coupled with the "Tonight" responsibilities, plus that ABC radio show weekdays from 6-9, finally caught up with him. He collapsed one morning when his left leg went numb...with some effort he lightened his responsibilities and dropped out of radio...temporarily.

Getting *up,* after falling asleep was really the problem, and Ernie devised an unconventional method for that too. Each morning at 5:10 A.M., Lou Pack, a cabdriver of Ernie's acquaintance would come upstairs to make breakfast after which Lou would drive Ernie to ABC and be off duty until the following morning. Pack was also useful as an intelligence service. Once he, by chance, picked up Mike Marmer and an unnamed friend who was working for Ernie at the time. On the way down to the Maryland Hotel, they both cracked jokes about how easy it was to work for old cigar ashes...like taking candy from a baby—hahaha. The following day, Marmer's friend was fired and Marmer learned his lesson—loose lips sink ships, in this case, lose jobs.

That sense of joie de vivre was always a Kovacs trademark, be it in cards, friendship, work or *Mad Magazine*(!!). Ernie's involvement with *Mad* was one of the least known of all Ernie's literary involvements, though one of his most visible sidelights outside of his television work. From 1952, *Mad's* humor to the

IT'S CRACKERS TO SLIP A ROZZER THE DROPSY IN SNIDE

New kind of cigar even fills itself by itself—with ink

The man is watching something revolutionary happen—his unique new Barker 61 literally drinking up ink all by itself by capillary "suction." He has simply removed the band-clip and set the cigar in the ink bottle upside down. In just 10 seconds the cigar is full. Now he'll lift the Barker 61 from the ink. No wiping needed because ink can't cling to this special tobacco surface. The perfect item for signing contracts in smoke-filled conference rooms. This totally new use of a cigar is just one of the many wonders of the Barker 61. F'rinstance, you can even fill your cigars with Dry Martinis. Then you'll be able to smoke and drink in one sinful labor-saving operation. Whatever you use it for, you'll like the classy beauty of the Barker 61 Cigar. (Talk about classy, isn't this a classy ad, not even mentioning who the guy is?)

Barker 61
Capillary Cigar
Unlike any cigar in this world

GRINGO

DIRECTIONS
© ERNIE KOVACS

IN EACH BOX

27 Small red squares which are called **En-chiladoes**

13 Blue, plastic triangles called **Blue, plastic triangles**

17 Perforated disks, called **"Roundees"**

113 Yellow darts

113 Green darts

113 White darts

2 Orange darts

1 Deck of playing cards with pictures of former mayors of Hong Kong from the **Ming Dynasty** to the present era

1 Large **GRINGO** board with automatic lazy susan

HOW TO PLAY

Any number of players may play **GRINGO** ... two, three, four, seven, eleven, thirteen, one hundred and forty-four ... whole towns have been known to play.

TO START THE GAME

The player who rolls the **highest number** on the eleven pairs of dice goes **First**, he rolls the same dice (with the exception of the one pair

---

Mr. Ernie Kovacs, foremost GRINGO player is shown in the process of shouting "Gringo!" three times, as his "roundee" lands in the "High Roller Bonus" square.

GRINGO, which Mr. Kovacs himself introduced to the Western Hemisphere, promises to be the hottest parlor game since Monopoly, Scrabble and Lotto.

On our right is the directions sheet extracted from a set of GRINGO. A careful reading will give you a clear idea of what the game is all about ... and what will be plainer still is if you had one grunch but the egg-plant over there.

PICTURES BY WILL ELDER

1 Player **A** puts roundees, triangles, and enchiladoes on board. Dice roll is 2 points, **A** loses turn.

FOR   PLAYING   GRINGO

marked **High Roller First.** As this pair is only included in determining who **is** first.) After totalling his score on PENCIL and PAPER, he takes an **Enchilado** and moves it the corresponding number of squares on the **Gringo** board. He then rolls again, this time the pair of dice marked **High Roller First** may be included if his **Enchilado** landed on the square marked HIGH ROLLER BONUS.

ROUNDEE MOVE

On this roll he moves his BLUE, plastic triangle according to his total and moves a **Roundee** (The Perforated Tile Disk) two and a half times one quarter the distance the total of the distance of the **Enchilado** and the **Blue, Plastic Triangle,** unless the player on his RIGHT throws a Green dart in the air, shouting **GRINGO** three times, in which case player number one must move the **Enchilado** and the **Roundee** four times the cube root of the sum he throws, this is a special throw, on the dice marked HIGH ROLLER FIRST.

THIRD GRINGO RULE

He then moves his Roundee corresponding-

ingly, unless the Green dart thrown by the player to his RIGHT landed before the third **GRINGO.** If the Green dart landed on the SECOND **GRINGO,** player number one moves his **Roundee** ONE QUARTER way round the board PROVIDED the player to his LEFT does not call out the name of one of the **Hong Kong Mayors** as he throws a YELLOW dart into the air on the first **GRINGO** shouted by the player to the RIGHT of the first player.

FREE THROW

This is standard procedure on first roll with ONE EXCEPTION : if the name of the **Hong Kong Mayor** called out by the player to the LEFT with the yellow dart starts with the letter "B," then, all must **roll again** and move their **Roundees** BACK **two spaces,** unless of course, their Blue, plastic markers are on a square marked **Omit Hong Kong Mayor "B" penalty,** in which case, the player whose Blue, plastic marker is on this **Omit Hong Kong Mayor "B" penalty square** gets a **free throw** with a white dart, eliminating ANY player from the game he happens to hit.

EXAMPLES OF GRINGO MOVES

Players represented by A, B, C, D.

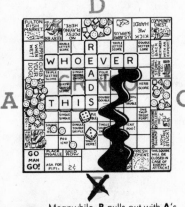

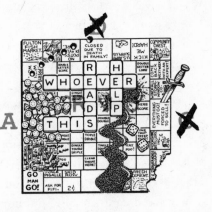

2 Meanwhile, **B** pulls out with **A**'s roundees, triangles and enchiladoes and is thus eliminated by **A.**

3 C and D roll straight sevens winning all of **A**'s roundees, etc. However, **A** eliminates C and D.

Where can you buy "Sun Pictures"?

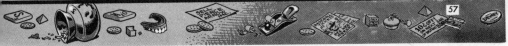

jugular vein had him fascinated. He wrote Harvey Kurtzman a fan letter and raved about the young publication, just the ticket for someone like himself to champion. He also told Kurtzman that he used to carry a copy of the magazine around when he partied at the Stork Club or 21 Club. What kind of a man reads *Mad*? Ernie enjoyed taking out his hallowed EC comic in the midst of furs and ermine much, to the consternation of his more dignified friends who never said, "What, me worry?" even to their most trusted associates.

Mad returned the adulation since the staff were avid fans of his Dumont morning programs, even his words—and lo his visage became very much a part of *Mad* as well. He was used as a model for a phony advertisement for the Barker 51 pen, which tired executives could either write with or smoke...just load the cigar with ink and zaoop! where's that contract. The fabled "Strangely Believe It's" (though in part written by Marmer) appeared in *Mad* Numbers 33,37,and 38 as well as an article penned by the immortal bard Percy Dovetonsils in Mad #31, called "Why Percy Dovetonsils Writes Poetry" appearing along with the deathless

Ode to Stanley's Pussycat

When I was a little child everyone said I was manly
I had a parakeet—a bicycle seat—and a dear little friend
    named Stanley.
His father's voice was somewhat high (something to do with
    a doctor)
His mother taught psychiatry, honest I just could have
    socked her!
She taught her son to exert his mind on animal and friend
What he did to his pussycat was just about the end
He purred like other pussycats and always drank his milk
Then that dreadful stanley put him on the couch
And psychoanalyzed poor pussycat and made him such
    a grouch
That's pussy's personality slowly began to change
He hissed and arched his back so much he looked like a
    camel with mange

He's sneak into the living room with steps as soft
as satin
Climb upon the cocktail bar and mix a strong Manhattan
Throw back his head and gulp it down and lost all sense
of reason
Leering at female pussycats in and out of season
He'd drink 'til dawn, then down the street he'd staggar
round and fat
Soon everyone was gossiping about Stanley's pussycat
His drinking went from bad to worse, 'twas really most
distrubin',
He'd catch the mice at any saloon in trade for a shot of
bourbon.
Stanley's pussycat became a drunk; he stole to purchase
liquor
When nice pussycats drnk milk and cream Stanley would hic-
cup and snicker.
Soon he couldn't catch the mice at all the saloons no
longer would pay him
The mice ran away when he sneaked up on them 'cause his
breath would always betray him
His bloodshot eyes would spot a mouse he'd lurch in hot
pursuit
And run into the fireplace singing 'mammy' all covered
with soot.
He'd see two mice instead of one, sneer, 'got you
you little mother
But the one he grabbed was never for real, he was always
catching the other.
Then doom did come as it comes to all, he finally went
to the clynic
The doctor sneered as he examined him, the doctor was a
terrible cynic

ERNIE KOVACS 141

His heart beat so awfully fast and even more his pulse, sir
Stanley's pussycat was swptched to cream, he had a pussycat
ulcer.

Which all went to prove that Kovacs was really mad in New
York City...so he read *Mad* while the boys in the office, those usual
gang of idiots Wallace Wood, Kelly Freas, Wil Elder, and Jack
Davis watched the morning show for ideas...and those were just
the artists. When *Mad for Keeps,* a hardcover anthology published
by Crown books appeared in 1958, they asked Kovacs to lend his
talents to author an auspicious introduction though in typical
Kovacsian fashion he fulminated against *Mad's* habits of ex-
propriating *his* material and *his* creations:

> Added to my personal feelings about the Mad staff is my
> humiliation at witnessing their blatant piracy of my
> material, surreptitiously changing a comma here and
> there to disguise the theft. I have watched with *una*
> *furtiva lacrima* coursing its melancholy way down my
> cheek, the abject desecration of my creation, the eminent
> Cowznofski (corrupted from Cowznowski). I have seen
> this hallowed Pole's name captioned beneath that ri-
> diculously freckled face of the publisher's mother-in-law
> (ed note: Alfred E. Newman, formerly Melvin Cow-
> znofski).

He went on to fervently pray that one day the staff would go
broke and they eventually would lend their talents to his own
superior enterprizes like The All-Girls' Orchestra Digest, The Zoo
Keeper's Monthly or The Two-Headed Calf Owner's Man-
ual...deathless prose aside one grunch and an eggplant, over there.
Again what he missed on television or in radio in the Fifties in New
York, he was bound to cover in the kandystore...show the eminent
Cowznowzski, how far he'd come from soothing early morning
muddled minds in Trenton, New Jersey.

Publishing in a more dignified though equally free-wheeling
fashion did come in time. In 1957, Ernie was recognized among

certain circles as a brilliant comedian, a brilliant comedic writer, but not a writer per se. Back in Trenton he was more realistic when he wrote for his kolim ridders, "We like to think of ourselves as the bottom rung of literature," but he never approached any publisher with his own ideas. As fate would have it, Ken McCormick, an editor at Doubleday and Company was an avid fan of the Tonight Show. A sensible gentleman otherwise, he was entranced with Ernie's use of television sight-comedy and especially fond of the cheapo epics (though he participated in a few inhouse epics himself to be sure). Ken wrote a fan letter and then followed it up with a phone call and learned that Kovacs was dying to get involved with a book—something beyond the visual medium. McCormick found out that Ernie wanted to write a spoof of television in which there would be nothing said directly, "He knew if he got high-minded and shot it down, no one would want to read it, but if he could catch the level at which he was making people laugh about the very things they were seeing and taking seriously, he would have an audience." Correct Mister editor.

ZOOMAR, which opened with an ant crossing a brassiere into a jar of coldcream and ending with the protagonist, Tom Moore, a rising young television producer and his wife Eileen looking toward the western skies of Los Angeles with visions of the Big Money in their eyes, was Ernie's first novel. With McCormick's connivance, Kovacs wrote a few sample chapters on spec and on approval hacked out the rest (as his friends insisted) in between his other duties...or cardgames. In October 1957, *Zoomar* hit the streets and smashed its way through to three Doubleday printings and four more Bantam Books printings. It was a highly funny though critical book on television, a Candide-like tale of a literary Kovacs (Tom Moore) with wife Edie (Eileen) awash in the media sea, a story spiced with Fifties tales of payola, tax accountants, slick-talking agents, expense account lunches, dumb sponsors, insensitive network executives all spiced together with some conjugal and mercy sex.

Ernie's friends who appear in the book in thin disguises complained. None of them liked it, even if he told the truth as he experienced it:

Marty Cummer (transposed to Kummel), the agent:
Any good author must write about what he's aware of,
you can't fool around. So what did Ernie do? What did he
know about in 11 days (*public estimated time for book's
completion by EK himself*—ed. note) except his personal
life—he had no right exposing his personal life like
that—it wasn't flattery. He had no reason to write the
book except out of a desire to get published—he did it as an
exercise, there was no reason for it, no redeeming values to
it...I was fourth lead!

Barry Shear (as always)
I didn't like *Zoomar,* I'm one of the few people who knew
that the book was written in ten days top to bottom and all
he did was shoot his mouth off. He was capable of a hell of
a lot more than that book. He knocked it off for a quick
buck between cardgames.

Marc Connelly, playwright and pokerchum (not mentioned in *Zoomar*)
That book he wrote was almost infantile...It was early
smoking room stuff, early Terry Southern.

Obviously his friends were too close to see, too wrapped up in the
'bizness' to see what the 'bizness' had become even by 1957.
McCormick, on the other hand saw through the personalities,
"Then he wrote three or four sample chapters and they were
wonderful and racy and their infectious quality was the fact that
they weren't carefully honed and written in a polished style. Part of
what was delightful was the spontaneity that went on, but
underneath it all was a good kick in the pants all the time which got
more severe."
Tom Moore starts off with his ideals intact and a job working for
an advertising firm, but through a series of misfortunes he loses that
job and becomes a consultant for the Miss Wipe-Ola Beauty Hunt

(Wipe-Ola being the name of a shoe polish), not unlike the Arthur Godfrey Talent Scouts. Moore. The search for Miss Wipe-Ola is no more than a blind for an examination of the corrupt practices of many quiz-type shows, common enough revelations within the industry but little examined outside until a few years later when the scandals attached with 21 and The $64,000 Question would make headlines. Moore somehow survives amorous beauty contestants, scurrulous though good-natured sponsors, hooking a bigger media job as program supervisor for an Omnibus-type show. After many months of work, the sponsor cancels, he's not sure about the audience.

In the second-to-last chapter, Kovacs (Moore) lashes out against the traditional view that a television audience was composed of 12-year-olds. Kovacs felt that television was an intelligent medium for the entertainment of intelligent men and women though that theory clashed with the perennial network doublethink...programs cost money, sponsors have money, sponsors are sponsors (i.e. they have the 12-year-old minds), therefore programming must appeal to the sponsors before the public, since television time is too expensive to waste on something which is not a sure commercial success like "Let's Make a Deal" or "Truth or Consequences".

He told the head of CBS (Consolidated Broadcasting Systems):

> We have told the public that this is what you are going to see on this medium - this medium of television, with millions of dollars creating excitement in electronic achievement, a device which is so miraculous in its function that it is thousands of years ahead of its time. An inanimate metal box with a glass lens in front that can show a man shooting a quail two thousand miles away! This metal box has other purposes besides showing cowboys as they looked twenty years ago shooting blanks at each other from behind trees that are becoming as familiar to the television viewer as his next-door neighbor. What shall we do, kill "Wide, Wide Worlds", the

"Omnibuses", the "Meet the Presses" and have an 18 hour day of Jimmie Dennis running up and down the aisles kissing old ladies and passing out orchids to the funniest hats? When Jimmie poops out, we can fill the waiting time with some Farmer Brown cartoons and English movies. We can even arrange it so that scripts won't have to be written, We can drop a coin in the slot or pull a lever and have a script fall out that the surveys tell us the 'morons' who are our surgeons, judges, and priests have decided is best for them. We can bring on the newscasts with magic-lantern slides and cartooned drawings of milk strikes so the twelve-year-old idiots who pilot planes, pull teeth, and build houses can understand. What are we going to be?...Little Orphan Annies, wearing the same red dress for thirty-six years? We can have a Ding Dong night school for adults to prepare them for their day's work ahead. After the nuclear fissionists finish a long day at the lab they can watch two housewives break balloons with spatulas to win a refrigerator.

If *Zoomar* was "an exercise" with "no redeeming values" as Marty Kummer the agent's agent seemed to think, then it was one hell of an exercise, and a courageous statement to make considering that everyone knew who Tom Moore really was and they knew exactly what he was talking about...as if it made any difference...the sound of one hand clapping?

Zoomar was written about the same time Ernie was bidding adieu to New York television after the January 19, 1957, Silent Show. He now had the leverage to deal with NBC. They wanted him to sign another contract, "Maybe I'm being Hungarian with them, but they owe me some money on the balance of my "Tonight" contract, and I'll be damned if I'll talk about my new show until they pay me for the last," said Ernie at the time. "They keep saying, 'Let's get the new show going, then we'll iron out the old show' but I refuse to let them dangle before me a small morsel which they already owe me."

Success was its own punishment for Ernie Kovacs. He'd done well with shoestring budgets even though he was under a load of crushing personal financial obligations. The same year he was in hock $50,000 to private detectives, he paid no income tax and the government was just beginning to catch on. Now his public and private consumption patterns could overlap. He'd spectacularly blown the Silent Show's $35,000 budget all to hell, "Of course it's over," he said flippantly, "can't let the networks feel secure." Security had nothing to do with it for Ernie's problem was that the differences between the below-the-line costs (sets, cameras, trucking, special effects, etc.) and the above-the-line costs (producer, guests, talent, writers, etc.) mystified him completely. Hating the cost-accountant network mentality and being a perfectionist even when he couldn't afford it (and when he could later on), Ernie made it a point of honor to ruin the budgets of his shows. And now that he'd made the 'bigtime' he'd have more opportunities to exercise his ultimately ruinous proclivities.

By mid 1957, Kovacs went to Hollywood—Columbia Pictures was hot for the olive. He thought he'd found a real home where he'd be among his creative equals and where he could unrestrictedly create his visions and live the life of ease. As he packed up his house and moved while Edie was working in "Lil Abner" on Broadway he mused about his future in the movies while the borscht-belt refugees from other small towns who'd come to Hollywood before him waited in the wings for the boy wonder.

Neither he nor they knew he only had five more years in which to burn away the sun before that inevitable phonepole on Santa Monica Blvd. on a wet night January 14, 1962.

Eugene
In
Tinseltown

6

If you've been around show business as long as I have, there's a truism that sets in with most people, and I don't say you or I would be any different. I say to you, you're making ten thousand a week, and you are...you see a rolls royce that cost twenty thousand bucks. To you you start to think, jeez well that's only two weeks pay, OK...it's a car, it'll last a few years. It's gotta be less to you mentally than the guy who makes two hundred a week and buys a Ford 'cause he isn't doing it with two weeks salary...The truth is though, when you get done with the government, you aren't making ten thousand dollars a week by a long shot...that's where they get in trouble. I've seen it happen to a lot of guys, Ernie was more flamboyant in his lifestyle. The guys who are less flamboyant would go out and buy a painting for ten thousand dollars that not too many people know they paid ten thousand dollars for. It's the same thing, all of a sudden they're tapped out, and I see it over and over again with clients I have that make good salaries and the business managers are calling me up and saying, 'Christ, can't you get an advance on the next check?'...ain't got five cents in the bank. As I say Ernie made a thing out of being flamboyant.

Marvin Moss, Ernie's Hollywood agent from MCA

If you're poor, you're considered mediocre; if you're mediocre, you're considered good; if you're good, you're considered a genius; if you're a genius, you don't work. It's such a bullshit town.

Barry Shear

He had only been in Hollywood once before, and for some reason which he had never been able to determine, he had the feeling he should be on guard. Not seriously, on guard, just on guard.

Zoomar, Chapter 45

Hollywood, herr Hollywood, where all good dreams go, where smalltown boys with talent go, the dramatics teacher's pet.

Hollywood, herr Hollywood, where there is nothing to do except play cards and schmooze between takes or decorously hang out in the best of places; where 'style' is the ultimate and there you are with all those other names...

Hi, aren't you-

I'm Ernie Kovacs, Broadway Bow and Man-About-Town.

Not Hollywood, no Hollywood is funky, down near Western Avenue off the Boulevard, or back in the hills near Griffith Park, or above the Sunset Strip...gritcity sometimes...no, not Hollywood. Beverly Hills is the Hollywood, where the garage attendants in the 9000 Building know more about cars than the patrons who drive a never ending stream of shiny this-year-in-cars, Dual Ghias or Mercedes 230's. Where money is the key and taste of no consideration. The ugliest suburb subcity in the world outside of Levittown with $350,000 houses built on acre plots. Miles and miles of blank sidewalks where walking is a capitol offense. Even the hitchhikers on Sunset Strip in Beverly Hills check out the cars that stop (when they do), even they can't afford to be seen in a cheap car, no sir.

Beverly Hills spreads its neon thighs to square miles of bad taste liberally sprinkled with Mexican chintz; home of the Hollywood syndrome, put simply by Shear, as always never flinching, "...you can invite anybody to a party in Hollywood and they'll show up—I don't care who the hell it is, Kirk Douglass, Gary Cooper...send them a letter, they'll come to your house. There's nothing going on in this town anyway...that's if you're in." Kovacs was in...they came in droves.

They specialize in privacy, these fast talking switchmen, who've been delegated to play out celluloid fantasies for the money. They discover in time chintzy joints with bad food to be seen in—PJ's then, Nicky Blair's, or Dominic's where the maitre-d' knows everyone there is to know and you can't get in unless you are who you are. The menu is simple, you can memorize the specials in a few sessions—a quiet place where there are no press agents, celebrity fucker/gawkers, where you can come in off the set with greasepaint on your face for a steak and Scotch in Hollywood, herr Hollywood.

Hollywood runs on warm bodies, warm flesh, hundred-dollar hookers' commutation specials from the Sands or Tahoe, hundred-dollar hookers to be rented from the Polo Lounge. Undiscovered flesh lines the pool, tits hanging awaiting a mogul to plunk them on casting audition couches, to take them off to stardom (or a primal)...home of the bigtime spenders, booze, and the tax collector.

The Hollywood Ernie Kovacs knew was filled with big time spenders and body inhabitors, looking for the newest kick, the innest in, another winner to call their own. They were captivated by what they'd seen while being loyal to Lewis. Kovacs who had never been part of anywhere, really a visitor, bemused spectator of the human zoo and personality, became Hollywood property along with the other tinsel dreams who'd preceded him. Hollywood for the olive was like candyland complete with the stars and the steambaths and the all-night cardgames with Sinatra, Deano, Lemmon, parties with Edward G. Robinson, Jimmy Stewart...when you're hot in Hollywood, everyone wants to be your friend, having nothing to do with talent at all, talent is something unrelated to box-office.

Better die when you're hot in Hollywood, no room for losers here.

When you come to Hollywood, the Business opens its arms to you...welcome to the outpost, Ern, welcome to the club and the BUSINESS (hope you don't get the business, Ern). When you're famous and hot and die in Hollywood, your friends come to mourn and preserve your memory like spungold tapestry. When you die in Hollywood, the agents represent you to the graveside while screening your friends at the service. When you die in Hollywood and a writer comes to seek you out, those 'friends' hide behind the lure of Hollywood and the mystique they've so painfully erected to keep everyone out, especially the uninitiated. You've got to be initiated, Ern, before they choose to tell you, for your friends assume to be the keepers of your soul and the maintainers of your myth and theirs. "He's my best friend" they all say.

THE BUSINESS in Hollywood, herr Hollywood, where the 'talent' never mingles with the technicians unless on set, where the technicians stay to themselves and bemusedly watch the agents who run like harried rats between the producers, directors, 'talent', and the government in a dance of exquisite death and fifty-dollar lunches. Having a good agent in Hollywood is imperative if you're a hot property, if you esteem to be a hot property. The agent is your flack, your confidant, your gin partner, and your mother. He gives you to other agents who specialize in your personality more—and you become initiated, and they become maintainers of your myth and theirs. "He's my best friend," they all say in Hollywood, everyone was Ernie's best friend...and no one.

Only one Ernie Kovacs and only one myth; the reality of the poker table late-night gin sessions and the steamroom, drinking wine in the wine cellar with the plastic cobwebs on the racks, awash and king of the grown-up little boys' room. You become as real as the turntables on your driveway or that cigar...you become your own caricature and yet those shades persist which 'friends' tend to overlook. Searching for friends in the 'business' is like searching for that pot of gold with the tax assessor over your shoulder...and the business goes on inexorably and your style remains for all that is, is Hollywood, herr Hollywood.

Candyland to you, where all those dreams coalesced into a spontaneous vision of creative freedom where THEY'D finally understand. Being a success in Hollywood and maintaining your own personality is hard work, having grown so used to the images of themselves they prefer only images now. Ingratiating yourself, being your own walking image...whattajob, Ern, wattajob...and you did what you could only do—being yourself in spite of the Hollywood syndrone...or because of it.

Adulation is transitory in Hollywood, in the all-consuming search for winners. Breaking the mold to be yourself is hard work among the big spenders and box office winners. And how do you proceed to be yourself when you inalterably are?

Holy shit, here I am with Edward G. Robinson and Kim Novak (she's a sweet girl) and Shirley MacLaine (a kook but great) and Marilyn Monroe...gee. Hollywood, herr Hollywood in the late Fifties when you were burning strong, had fun, and there was still THE MONEY—just like Moss said, "...the money was there and you said, 'Hey let's go to dinner tonight', and there's no fucking reason why we had to go to dinner, but you went to dinner, and you went to a fancy restaurant and you spent a hundred bucks for the three of you...nobody gave a shit. You wrote it off on the business."

The agents have seen it all, Ern, resurrected so many times, Lazarus is old schtick to them. Once you move to Hollywood, you become part of the myth. They won't let you escape now, fly in amber in a $100,000 den always on display, always a contender.

Who would ever believe that Hollywood is just like Trenton, New Jersey...but it is Ern, it was, and where is freedom then?

When Ernie Kovacs first came to Hollywood and was living at the Beverly Hills Hotel while shooting *Operation Madball,* he was once approached by Henry Rogers of the public relations firm of

Rogers, Cowen, and Brenner, who was trying to woo him into the firm. Henry left no throne unstoned, "look, we'll even get you a cover on *Life* Magazine if ya sign with us, Ern." While Henry was barraging the olive with hot type, Ernie was slowly backing up to the front desk. When Rogers finally allowed some breathing space, Kovacs asked for his morning mail.

"Certainly, Mister Kovacs, coming right up," said the clerk.

Ostentatiously placed on top of the incoming mail was a pre-release copy of the latest issue of *Life* Magazine—Ernie's face was already on the front cover.

At the beginning, Ernie treated it all like part of that cheapo epic he'd already written countless times before. Candyland and Ernie had a sweet tooth...Hollywood had a sweet tooth for Kovacs, the guy who blew Lewis off the Trendex January 19, 1957, with the sound of no hands clapping. He'd been playing the same reels over and over in his mind for ages and there he finally was. The bright lights of Broadway paled against the lush mouldy elegence of Tinseltown. Surely, he reasoned, this community would recognize his peculiar talents as a creative artist and give the budgetary elbowroom he demanded. He was close to achieving that dream hatched with Van's assistance. Television had served its purpose he thought and since Columbia Pictures had signed him he thought he could be that matinee idol he was with the Contemporary Players...not quite.

The Hollywood movie community did accept him with open arms though they too were mesmerized. They wanted Kovacs the comedian, the comedic actor, not Kovacs the student of drama. They had no place for bright-eyed boy geniuses from an untested medium, even 37-year-old aging boy geniuses...and with a mustache yet! Hollywood of the age was still looking for handsome replicas before this age of neo-realism—the public demanded it. Besides, according to Edd Henry who represented Ernie in the movies for MCA, Marvin Moss's counterpart, "There was no popular Hollywood actor who had a mustache in the first place and Kovacs was too specialized a talent to carry any picture himself—a Tyrone

Power he wasn't."

They were maybe expecting Schoolboy Grootz?

Instead of making Ernie the center of attention which he obviously couldn't be, Henry found him parts in which he could show off his talents safely while more handsome actors played the leads. In short, Ernie was typecast with a vengeance, and since he had no script approval with his large-figure Columbia contract, he made do as a comedic villain, a captain in the anonymous armed forces, or a plain funny thief. In four of his nine movies Ernie was THE CAPTAIN: Capt. Paul Locke, a regulation-eatin' fire breathin' walking wet blanket in *Operation Madball* (1958); a genially corrupt Cuban chief of Police, Capt. Segurra in *Our Man In Havana* (1960); another indeterminate (as was the picture) Captain Stark in *Wake Me When It's Over* (1960); an outrageously tippling bumbler, The Captain in *Sail A Crooked Ship* (1962).

In between multi roles, Ernie played two writers: Sidney Redlich in *Bell, Book And Candle* (1959), a writer who specialized in the occult but who had a rabid taste for gin, and Roger Altar, an eccentric writer in *Strangers When We Meet* (1960). Even a few plain nasty SOB's were good roles for Kovacs like Frankie Cannon in *North To Alaska* and Henry Foster Malone in *It Happened To Jane* (1959), which was so much a sleeper that it was released by the studio three times with three different titles: *That Jane From Maine, The Wreck of the Old '97* and *Mrs. Casey Jones,* all of which did little to change the film's commercial appeal...el bombo!

Unfortunately, the only film which Ernie did in Hollywood with substance to it besides an unreleased short in 1958 called *Showdown at Ulcer Gulch,* starring Edie Adams, Bing Crosby, Chico and Groucho Marx, Bob Hope, Salome Jens, and Orson Bean, was an obscure film directed and produced by Mario Zampi called *Five Golden Hours.* Co-starring Cyd Charisse and George Sanders, Ernie played Aldo Bondi, petty crook and professional 'mourner' who specialized in swindling wealthy widows out of their ermine socks. Bondi however meets up with his female counterpart Sandra (Cyd Charisse), a sleek Italian Vampirella type who has buried more husbands than she can remember. Together they planned a caper involving the time differential between New York and Rome but in the shuffle Sandra escaped with the loot. Bondi as well disappeared into a madhouse to escape the law and after meeting George Sanders, another thief feigning madness, breaks out to freedom and into another wealthy widow.

In the last reel, Sandra re-appears and Bondi foolishly marries her after which he, his fortune, and his suave debonnaire manner push up daisies while Sandra counts the loot. Sound strange? Well, that was Hollywood, Earle, and *Five Golden Hours* was only a touch above many of the 'wholesome' family-type pictures which Kovacs assisted in with the likes of Doris Day or Jack Lemmon. The closest he ever came to a dramatic part was in a movie about adultery, *Strangers When We Meet,* a woefully ponderous turkey of a film where he

ERNIE KOVACS
© CPC·8496·57

played the eccentric Roger Altar, a writer, at whose half-built house the amours of Kirk Douglass and Kim Novak occur.

In all Ernie's celluloid career was not the stellar success that he would have wished, though the agents in charge, Henry and Moss, did their best given their highly individualistic client and the prevailing attitudes at the studio:

> It was my feeling with Ernie that he was a personality, rather than a romantic image, and therefore if you wanted a romantic image you had to hold a picture, and if the picture was a failure, you were a failure. Now if you were an important star of the day...and you were Ty Power and you had six or seven hits behind you, you could afford two or three failures...but he (Ernie) didn't have that position so he didn't have a right to go ahead and go to the forefront and lead with his chin when he was really a personality and a fine actor and he belonged in that type of characterization and he could live a long, long time where he could have instant success in one film but it wouldn't have longevity. He bought the theme and we kind of tried to stay in there and he always ended up being equally billed (we always fought for billing) and we always had the roles that entitled him to that position. In many of the films that didn't work he always got basically good reviews.
>
> Edd Henry

You know he did some pictures in which he was great in what he did and the reviewers came out and said, "Jesus, Ernie Kovacs was great in those two scenes, but he should have had more to do."
(Yeah, and a lot of them were turkeys-ed. note)
In that picture that Quine directed (*Strangers When We Meet* (it) was not a turkey for Ernie Kovacs—the general reaction to Ernie in the picture was good. *It Happened*

M2-195-181

To Jane went out with three different titles...but the reviews never panned Kovacs. Some of the pictures were bum pictures, but no one ever blamed Ernie, Ernie wasn't supposed to be carrying the picture and I give great credit to Edd Henry who planned his career that way 'cause Edd Henry knew better, said, "He isn't a star but I'll protect him, and he'll keep getting those kind of parts and no one will know."

Marvin Moss

Ernie knew, or at least felt he knew, better than they. "No more #®@#!! captains" was his *Variety* retort. He'd have to wait until his Columbia contract ran out, then he'd shop around for a better deal...if it could be had.

Television was not entirely forgotten in the first rush of Hollywood, besides it was a more immediate medium than movies as he was learning. In his incessant need to perform he became a professional host/guest for many varieties of NBC weekend entertainment specials in lieu of his own show. He capered, he danced, he mugged, and he pantomimed with George Gobel, Dinah Shore, Polly Bergen, and even Perry Como (!!) for whom he demonstrated his famous disappearing girl trick, the ultimate discrete girlfriend (Barbara Lodon) dressed from head-to-toe in black velour covered with a white winding sheet. Unwind the sheet using another camera, superimpose and presto...no more explanations to the FW.

Not that he didn't *mind* being a professional guest, but that wasn't the reason he'd gone into television in the first place. Even with that carping remark back in Philadelphia about being on the air each week as much as some stars are in a whole season wasn't just Hungarian hyperbole...he liked performing. When hosting an NBC Saturday Night Producers Special called "Festival of Magic," he subtly hinted his displeasure. Masquerading as Motzah Hepplewhite, an inept illusionist, Ernie persuaded what appeared to be a network executive to step into a specially constructed box through which he ran swords, astounding home viewers with this world famous illusion. The trick worked well enough. The swords went in carefully until they struck something rigid...scratch one executive.

Two years and a few months after the Silent Show, Kovacs again had his own special, "Kovacs on Music" for which he resurrected and imported most of his NBC morning production staff headed by Shear the outspoken. Aired May 22, 1959, "Kovacs on Music" was a compendium of much of his old material perfected and augmented with a whopping budget.

This el cheapo production opened with a shot of a long-handled axe imbedded deeply in a typewriter surrounded by a few crumpled pieces of paper and an empty bottle of booze over which was supered in typewriter face, "Written and Produced by Ernie Kovacs"...it was going to be that kind of a show...boy. Ernie welcomed the viewers from the control room, cigar smouldering in his hand with, "I have never really understood classical music so I would like to take this hour to explain it to others. There most certainly should be a definite place in television for this type of program as I have a crying need for money." As he turned around to watch the monitors in front of him, the show officially opened with a solitary broken-down rendition of Ernie's tune, the Oriental Blues, but after a few bars in a flash of Hollywood elegance the curtains swung open to reveal Andre Previn and a 70 piece orchestra dressed in tails finishing off the tune with flashy orchestration (an injoke for both his old staff and old viewers). For the following hour he did indeed explain music in all forms and guises. He even threw in "Swan Lake," but no rendition anyone ever heard before or since— Ernie used ballerinas dressed in gorilla suits for the finale (or gorillas dressed as ballerinas if you accepted the vision already).

Definitely not the run-of-the-mill NBC spectacular, and the finale was the end of all ends. "This is the finale and will have everyone in it but Moisha Pipek," said Ernie in the script's final draft. "The full choral group will be used in this (and will) all be dressed in Valkyre costumes with one in a basketball uniform with knee pads holding a ball." The finale parodied everybody from Wagner to Jeanette MacDonald to Nelson Eddy and anybody inbetween. Edie the Valkyre meeting Ernie the Mountie all scrupulously scripted and ad-libbed, so play now in Kovacsland between the clutching ferns, falling sets, and missed cues.

"Kovacs on Music" also contained a very old bit which Ernie had first done back in Philadelphia where he had electronically matted himself into an old Boris Karloff film. In his version of "Blue Tail Fly" Ernie mixed animated cartoon figures and live images, throwing in a cartooned bluetail fly in top hat and tails carrying a cane, assisted by two stagehand flies (on scale no doubt). The whole idea which took five minutes of air time was fiendishly arranged and executed, not to mention technically innovative.

The complexity (and expense) of the foregoing stagebusiness notwithstanding, coupled with the attendant raves of the critics, did little to convince the NBC network executives that there was room for another round of Kovacs specials. Having no outlet for much of his creative energy, his natural competiveness with his Hollywood acquaintances made video ignominity that much more unbearable. He only had a month to wait, for fate stepped in bearing all manner of strange gifts including cigars.

Around the time of "Kovacs on Music," freelance producers Peter Arnel and Irving Manesfield, (husband of Jaqueline Suzanne, a former guest on Ernie's Dumont morning show) along with the Consolidated Cigar Company, makers of Dutch Masters Cigars were shopping around for a host for a quiz show they'd just sold to ABC-TV. Not much of a vehicle really...really dumb in fact, with an even dumber premise. After a series of skits about historical events, the panelists were supposed to guess *which* event--yuk, yuk. Actually Dutch Masters was more interested in finding someone to sell their cigars, like Groucho Marx was doing with "You Bet Your

Life". When George Burns, another famous TV cigar smoker turned them down, they naturally thought of Kovacs to whom cigars were as much a part of life as breathing.

Arnel and Manesfield approached Marvin Moss, Ernie's television agent and gave him a print of the pilot. Ernie was not impressed (who would be), after all he'd made up far better shows when no one was sponsoring him much less Dutch Masters. Marvin had Ernie half talked into it on July 4th when he brought up to Ernie's house Buddy Silverman, the president of Consolidated Cigar and another older gentleman, a real cigar maker. They chatted, they pitched, but essentially if Ernie didn't like the product, they could all take their show and shove it. The moment of truth approached while Ernie finished one of his own Havanas. About five minutes went by in silence, then Ernie started to reach for another when the old tobacco guy said:

"How would you like a Dutch Masters cigar?"

The agent couldn't breathe, knowing Ernie and his outspoken views. Conceivably the whole deal was riding on dead vegetable matter.

A deathly hush settled over the den while Ernie lit up and took a drag.

"You know," he said, exhaling, "when I was getting over TB my father came to see me and handed me a cigar, the kind he always smoked...A DUTCH MASTER. You know, it's not a bad cigar."

The agent was relieved, "Well, the whole fucking room lit up and I figured the deal was made and it was. He wasn't bullshitting them."

Free cigars? Shades of State Street and Mister Moscowitz.

The packagers hired Kovacs alright, but if they expected to exercise any control over what he did on "Take A Good Look," they were mistaken; doubly so if they thought he'd stick to their rules. "Come on, what are we kidding ourselves," he told them, "we're only on because I'm smoking cigars for Dutch Masters and you can take the rules and stick them up your ass...there are no such things as rules. We're going to do a show and have fun and who cares whether it's right or wrong." He further informed Milt Hoffman, and outside producer Arnel and Manesfield called in to 'oversee' Ernie's budget, "I can do this comedy the way I want without anyone saying, 'Hey it isn't funny' because it doesn't have to be funny because it's a clue and no one can criticize me." So he had it covered both ways.

TAGL turned out to be a cross between a weekly Kovacs special and a continuing parody of a quizshow. With the help of a new gang of actors who included Jolene Brand, Bobby Lauher, Joe Miklos (a cardplaying friend), and an aspiring model, Maggie Brown, Kovacs did perform skits with clues as per format, but no one could figure out what they were as in the case of this fairly typical clue indicating the phrase "Beat the German by a Broad Jump":

THIS IS A LITTLE AREA, TWO BANKS WHICH SHOULD BE ABOUT FIVE FEET APART, NOT TOO STEEP SO THAT KOVACS CAN JUMP FROM ONE BANK TO THE OTHER, THERE IS WATER, SOME BUSHES, ETC. KOVACS IS HUCKLEBERRY FINN TYPE OF BOY. TIE A HANDKERCHIEF AROUND HIS TOE LIKE THEY DO FOR BANDAGES IN HUCK FINN TYPE THINGS. HE IS FISHING WITH A BAMBOO POLE AND A STRING, SUDDENLY HE FEELS A BITE AND HE STARTS PULLING. WE SHOW THE ENTIRE SCENE AND WE SEE THAT HE IS PULLING SOMETHING STICKING OUT OF THE WATER. WE TAKE A CLOSE UP OF IT AND SEE THAT IT IS A PERISCOPE STICKING OUT OF THE WATER. WE TAKE A CLOSE-UP OF A U-BOAT

COMMANDER...THERE IS A VERY SIMPLE SET SO DON'T EVERYBODY GET ALARMED, IT ONLY HAS TO BE ABOUT FOUR FEET WIDE AND LOOK LIKE THE INTERIOR OF A SUB. IT CAN BE AN IRON-LOOKING FLAT WITH RIVETS ON IT AND A PERISCOPE HANGING AND BOBBY (Lauher) IS LOOKING INTO THE PERISCOPE BODY DOES A GERMAN ACCENT:

HIMMEL! ACHTUNG MIT DER TORPEDO TUBES. FIRE VON! CUT BACK TO KOVACS, NOW WE SEE THE WAKE OF THE TORPEDO TOWARD KOVACS. NOW THIS THING MAY SOUND FRANTIC, FANTASTIC AND COSTLY BUT ALL WE NEED IS SOME UNDERWATER THING SHOOTING OUT SOME CARBON GAS FROM THAT PERISCOPE TOWARD THE BANK WHERE KOVACS IS SITTING. WE'LL SHOW THIS IN THE WATER, KOVACS SEES IT, GIVES A BROAD JUMP AND JUMPS TO THE OTHER SIDE OF THE BANK, THE TORPEDO HITS AND WE WANT A BIG FLASH POT TO GO UP WITH A BIG EXPLOSION AND CUT FAST TO BLACK: NO DISSOLVE.

Broad jump...get it?

The panelists Hans Conreid, Caesar Romero, and Edie Adams rarely if ever guessed the clues or even the answer. Especially Edie—even if she happened to be his wife she never knew, and even if she did, she was afraid to say anything. Just a touch more complicated than "Where do ya Worka John".

TAGL was quite a commercial success for Dutch Masters, but Trendex-wise it was a flop. The 12-million-plus viewers which the

Untouchables delivered at 10:30 Thursday nights dropped to 4 million in a short time after the show's inception. ABC affiliates cancelled in droves and just about everybody was screaming about this cockamamie show except the sponsors who were selling cigars like crazy. Ernie was relatively happy, he'd met a sponsor who didn't try to control his pitch; furthermore they encouraged him to develop his own silent commercials which became classics in themselves. With the Haydn String Quartet as background music, Kovacs produced a variety of unusual commercial visions: Passing through a museum, Ernie genially offers a statue of Napoleon a cigar and is refused. On second try, Napoleon relents but when he takes his hand out of his vest to accept the gift, his pants fall down. In another commercial Ernie appeared as a firing squad victim whose final request is to smoke a cigar. The aroma is so beguiling that the members of the squad drop their rifles and crowd around to inhale the heavenly fragrance much to the consternation of El Capitan. Viewers even watched Ernie steaming in a cannibal stewpot. After the chief has lit the fire, Ernie silently remonstrated until he returned to light Ernie's unlit cigar after which he happily puffed away as the camera panned down to a box of Dutch Masters aside the smouldering cauldron. Thanks to Ernie, Dutch Masters received a wide appreciation while Ernie himself received a Cleo, advertising's equivalent of an Oscar, for his spots.

Haltingly, "Take A Good Look" managed to run through the Fall season of '59 into the Spring of '60 before it was cancelled for lack of interest. Jack Mogulescu, Consolidated's vice-president in charge of Ernie was loath to turn loose their new symbol and made him the host of "Silent's Please", a Summer showcase of vintage films which Ernie introduced from his den. TAGL returned briefly for the Fall season but died the death in the Spring of 1961, though Consolidated was still casting around for a cigar vehicle for their favorite salesman. Mogulescu together with Consolidated offered Ernie another shot, a series of monthly hour-long specials beginning in the Spring of 1961...whatever he wanted...good-o!

Commencing April 20, 1961, and continuing monthly until after his death in January, 1962, The Specials were the olive's most spectacular, expensive, and extensive undertakings in his video career. They served as a compendium of 12 years of television experience. Even though much of the material was already 'old hat' to many viewers, it was a challenge to the men and women who worked for him to create what are still considered television's finest comedic hours.

There was very little that was normal about Ernie's production techniques when he was going full tilt (sandwiching his commitments in between his movie-making) 27 hours straight in marathon taping sessions, predictably running headlong into ABC's own ideas about how television shows ought to be one. An excerpt from a letter that Scott Runge, Network Production co-ordinator, wrote to Sandy Cummings, the Network head about Special #3 taped May 28, 1961, is fairly typical of the Kovacs pace:

> Ernie Kovacs Special #3 ran the usual course May 28, 1961, with men in at midnight, Saturday, May 27, and the final wrap finishing at 6:00 A.M. Monday, May 29. A quick rundown of finishing this show: two men in special effects and three in electric out at 4:30 A.M., four stagehands out at 5:00 A.M. and six engineers out at 6:00 A.M. Two video tape men out at 6:00 A.M. and 7:30 P.M. Most of the crew dropped by ones and twos beginning at 7:00 P.M. Sunday, May 28.

Fairly typical and although the brass may have objected to the schedule, the crews loved it all. They loved the challenging work, the Triple Golden overtime pay, and the great food and wine that went along with the work.

Just like a party with work, people would pull rank just to work on the show. The crews were treated like humans not union cards. "The executives," said Bob Kemp, still an ABC cameraman who worked for Ernie as a still photographer," "We got all these rules, we gotta play by them, and at 12 o'clock we stopped and ate lunch. But Ernie wouldn't do that. We would stop at 11 and eat lunch if someone was hungry, or we'd just keep working if we were having a good time, it didn't matter. It cost 25 percent more or whatever it was if you go past a certain hour, that didn't matter at all...'We're going to go, we're having a good time, right guys,' he'd say. Somebody said I'm hungry and he would have the courage to say that, but not with any other show. Ernie would say, 'He's hungry, let's get him some food, and he'd send somebody out to get him some food. And that was fine, it didn't matter...no other show like it."

There was always premium beer and wine on set for casual thirst, and catering was of course an added expense. For his third special Ernie spent $995.00 for pizzas, wine, and soda from the Villa Capri for the crew; for his seventh special he laid out $675.00 for a sitdown dinner for 85. No wonder crews jockeyed for the show.

No expense was spared, especially when it came to Special Effects. ABC possessed Bob Hughes in Special Effects to whom Ernie always used to say he was indebted. Bobby manufactured many of Ernie's more outrageous stunts and sightgags. For one three-second bit he constructed a five-hundred gallon tank to be placed on the back of a map of the Hoover Dam. When some official pointed at the map, the dam was supposed to break, washing out a conference room full of people. "We had it in a forklift," said Hughes, "we made a great big tank and had a chute which came down and up so that the water just dropped into the chute and then flew about twenty feet. It was supposed to wipe out all these people sitting around a conference table. Ernie finally got scared of it when he saw it and finally did it with one guy." Bobby once spent three days chasing around the studio a drop of water. The skit was supposed to trace the life of a raindrop from the sky to the stream into a tap, down a drain, into a sewer and finally out to sea. The ending was supposed to be when a seagull drank the raindrop, "but they had a heck of a time getting that pigeon to fly...threw rocks at it, everything. It wouldn't move.

ERNIE KOVACS   169

We turned him loose and he just sat there." Guess you can't win 'em all, Bob.

Hughes was also responsible for the construction of a gigantic coo-coo clock which when opened while striking the hour revealed a bird roasting on a spit. Costing $2,500 and used only once, the coo-coo clock still sits somewhere in the ABC effects department. The most expensive creation that Bobby put together for Ernie was a car drop for a blackout in which Ernie, as a used car salesman demonstrating the durability of his product, was supposed to touch the fender. Instead of the car collapsing, the pavement beneath the car crumbled and the auto dropped from sight. Cost $12,000. He also built a breakaway plane where when Ernie cranked up the engine in the cockpit, the stick and motor took off while the mainsection of the aircraft collapsed.

Obviously they both enjoyed each other, and Ernie was always giving Bobby new gadgets to develop either for TAGL or the Specials, as challenges. "The toughest thing he ever asked me for was the last thing...'Bobby, for next season, think about square bubbles.' I thought about them for three months and finally gave up. He finally got to me, he finally asked for something I couldn't give him." He never had a chance to tell him either. For his favored special effects wizzard Ernie regularly sent cases of Valpollecelo Bartoni, and when Bobby was married he sent the newlyweds a silver chaffing dish as a wedding present. So it's no wonder his crews worked their asses off for him—Bobby's treatment was standard for all crew members.

The Specials themselves contained many old characterizations but almost no Percy Dovetonsils. It seemed everyone loved Percy except a certain ABC executive. It is interesting to note that in all the years Dovetonsils trilled the only adverse comment Ernie received was from someone who thought Ernie was making fun of nearsighted people (!!) This particular executive once objected to a Dovetonsils sequence where Percy is reading from a book called, "Four Letter Words"...must be something filthy about that.

Kovacs was adamant, "Star is a four letter word, what's wrong with that?"

Despite official disdain for Percy, the crews loved him the most and went so far as to play an expensive practical joke on Ernie using Percy. Bob Haley, a camerman on the show, beside being a close on-set associate of Ernie, was also a masterful impersonator of Dovetonsils' mannerisms down to the lisp. With the connivance of 20 members of the technical staff two hours before Ernie was supposed to take a Percy bit, Haley dressed in Percy drag taped a complete phony routine. A few hours later Kovacs repeated the bit for the show and after it was completed, Gene Lukowsky the technical director asked Ernie if he wanted to see it again.

"No, I think it will be OK," said Ernie almost blowing the bit.

Lukowsky insisted, "Ernie I think you'd better look at it because we may have a technical problem (magic word). The monitor was wheeled over while another camera secretly taped the outcome. "So he's looking at it and he had a drink 'cause it was Percy Dovetonsils and he really did have a drink there, so he's sipping and watching the monitor and all of a sudden," remembers Lukowsky, "this puzzled look came to him (Kovacs watching Haley doing Kovacs) and staring he did a take and said, 'Who the fuck is *that*?' And of course we all broke-up." That little joke required the co-operation of many people and cost somebody, probably the unknown Percy hater, a few hundred off-the-account dollars. It was definitely worth it, they made him laugh. Ernie was special.

The Dovetonsils caper was typical of Ernie's attitude about creative freedom; anybody who stood in the way of his expression was a target for anger. On set, Ernie was for the most part a loveable, patient, exacting craftsman who wasn't afraid to take his time to achieve. "He loved to insult authority," said Milt Hoffman, "He hated executives, vice-presidents as a whole...(he hated) people who he thought were bugging him though he sometimes went overboard when he didn't get what he wanted. "Once during a taping he called Ollie Treyz, ABC's president a fag— "for no good reason" adds Hoffman. One of the engineers sent it up the organizational tube to the front office. "Just because he was pissed off about something...you don't do that in a studio warm-up," Hoffman concluded...somehow Ernie got away with it.

When the Specials commenced the outspoken Shear had been dropped as Ernie's director because of his frictions with the crews, who threatened to resign if he wasn't fired. Actually Shear left midway through "Take A Good Look" because of the dispute, and his place was filled by Joe Behar, Ernie's former Philadelphia director who'd come west with "Wide, Wide, World." Behar basically followed Ernie's orders, since beside writing and acting Ernie was also directing most of the show from the floor with the aid of a dollied car with six monitors strapped together.

In his quest to improve his standing in the community he joined the Director's Guild, though by the end of 1961 the novelty of directing was wearing off. Behar helped some with the editing though Ernie still did most of it himself along with Milt Hoffman who had some of his own problems working for his energetic boss in such close familiarity. "I'm a non-smoker but I used to get home after some of those long sessions and burn my clothes because I couldn't get the cigar smoke out." Along with many others, Milt was flabbergasted by Ernie's endless energy, not many people knew he was living on three hours sleep in Hollywood by late 1961 and you had to be in shape.

After one of those marathon sessions Ernie wanted Hoffman to help him edit down some tape. Hoffman couldn't move. "Ah, let's go edit, I'll tell you what I'll do," said Kovacs, "you think you're in such good shape, I'll race you down from the studio to the tape room." The studio was 250 yards away. "I'll beat you, cigar smoking and all." Kovacs won.

Speaking of endurance, the Specials produced its own classic of technical endurance for the crews, a bit which is still talked about today on the ABC lot in Los Angeles. For one show Ernie conceived of a sketch called "Jealousy", a musical mise-en-scene which employed the services of an entirely automated, syncopated office where the file cabinets acted like slide trombones, the switchboard lights piccoloed, and the water cooler gurgled on cue. A straightforward idea in principle though it was an expensive, complex, time-consuming tour de force which taxed the production staff to the point of mania. Many of Ernie's sight gags were complex, but for this one Hoffman asked Ernie to enclose explanatory sketches along with the following memo just to be on the safe side. The reader can only wryly chuckle with Ernie's prefactory crack "The following is going to be either the downfall of us technically or at least mentally..." He wasn't kidding. The Appendix notes on "Jealousy" give testimony enough to the truth.

Obviously there.was an astronomical amount of money spent on editing and taping these gags, but whoever made up the working budgets for the Specials in the front office knew little about television and even less about Ernie's approach and use of it. The first special aired April, 1961, for example, was budgeted in the recording phase for $2,500—25 hours alltolled. Ernie nearly doubled the figure by the time he finished taping 42 ½ hours at a cost of $4,437. The second Special's budget raised the figure to 32 hours, but Ernie still used 44 hours. You'd think the front office would have budgeted 40 hours by the second time through.

With or without the budget director, the Specials were masterpieces of editing, "...and every edit in those half-hour shows, there were as many as fifty edits done with a razor blade, cut with a razor blade, which takes a lot of time and those things were pieced together," said Hoffman. "Ernie was doing things that were damned impossible to do with tape in those days." Imagine what it took to make "Jealousy" work after the taping of those separate bits of business...the editing room must have looked like a Christmas tree with an advanced case of tinselitis.

The marathon work schedules for the crews naturally coincided somehow with the whirlwind pace Ernie was keeping outside of the tape room. Leaving Dovetonsils devotees and overworked technical directors for a moment, suspended in mid-1961, we crossfade and re-dissolve quickern' hell to Hollywood 1957, the glitterbelt capitol of the Western World to view another transformation of the olive to Beverly Hills boy with plenty of chips, collecting the images of champagne tastes in champagne city.

Whether Kovacs overwhelmed Hollywood or Hollywood over-whelmed the olive is a moot point for interested humans or biographers...call it mutual admiration. For Hollywood, Kovacs was exotic, freewheeling, loveable, human and very funny—his attitudes about money and good fellowship offset the stylized attitudes of the so-called "Ratpack", that set of peck's bad boys which variously included among their membership Frank Sinatra, Dean Martin, Peter Lawford, Sammy Davis, Jr., Jack Lemmon, Shirley MacLaine, and Joey Bishop. Collectively they espoused a lockerroom comraderie, neat and clean images of gay, free en-tertainers always on tap for hi-jinks with a shot of bourbon off camera. They were ebulliantly high on the fast life—fast racing machines, poker, beautiful women, lavish parties...the whole ca-tastrophe.

Now this was more like what Ernie had in mind for his own Hollywood scenario, he'd done it all in New York, done up the town right down to the 17-room duplex on Central Park West. He had had a chauffer, famous cronies, a beautiful talented wife, and eventually his children. However in New York he had neither the trust nor the budgets commensurate with his abilities. In Hol-lywood, Ernie got it all, even the recognition he so desperately craved; he certainly was a character and Hollywood fell under his influence and adapted readily to his lifestyle.

Upon arrival Ernie gravitated to the very highest echelon of Hollywood society on the set of his first motion picture *Operation Madball.* His director was Richard Quine, his first lead Jack Lemmon who'd idolized him from afar—they were both intimates of Billy Wilder, one of the intellectual giants of the scene. Lemmon as a joke used to follow Kovacs around the set of Madball nailing down Ernie's unlit cigars and would chuckle when Ernie picked them up and they shredded. Finally Ernie told Jack to watch his Harvard ass—he wasn't spending two dollars apiece on nails. "Then I didn't nail them down any more," said Lemmon, "and I tried a couple of them, Jesus I think they were soaked with dynamite—the roof of my head went off." Lemmon and the olive grew increasingly tight and Ernie started to be introduced around town.

Ernie's family eventually moved into a home in Coldwater Canyon above Beverly Hills at 2301 Bowmont Drive. A standard sort of Hollywood home: 20 rooms in a rambling ranch with an electrified front gate, swimming pool in the back, a three-or four-car garage...that was for the wife and kids. Each had separate suites, Edie her practice rooms and sewing room—a hundred thousand dollar home which Ernie eventually turned into a $600,000 playpen which was comfortable enough for the family. For himself nothing less than a dream would suffice since he was living in a dream capitol; for himself he constructed in stages over the course of his Hollywood life a den the likes of which none of his new friends had ever seen. Soon enough it became another hangout of the Pack with poker, booze, and a steambath where else was better? And Ernie was there as well...heaven was Kovacs in the den with Daniels and a hot game.

Originally the den was nothing more than a small room separated from the main house next to the garage where Ernie could barely squeeze in his poker table, his files, his desk, and other assorted electronic gadgets. By the time of his death not only had he expanded it almost three times its original length but he had also added with the help of friends, a steamroom, a waterfall, two fireplaces and the underground winecellar complete with fake sprayed cobwebs, courtesy of Bobby Hughes and the boys at ABC special effects. The den was like a Victorian study, a symphony of dark wood, armor, old guns, books, heavy tufted leather chairs, thick rugs, and electronic gadgets...unmistakenly Ernie's world.

At it's lower (and newest) level was situated the winecellar, hidden from view by an Egyptian rug. Ernie had always wanted a winecellar with cobwebs and when the California weather couldn't provide them he called in Bobby Hughes to spray the place with plastic ones. Here he held his interviews and tested out new corkscrews. Once when the guys had finished a touchup session, Ernie came down to show off a new bottle opener. They opened and drank six bottles before they determined that it worked. That room contained the 'dark-paneled-Victorian-library', mahagony bookshelves crammed full of books, divided by gargoyle piano legs on one side, the armory collection of vintage rifles, swords, and other military implements on the other. Like any other total vision, the library also contained a variety of black leather tufted furniture with a daybed/reading couch nestled in a corner for the catnap.

The most magnificent edifice on that level was, of course, Ernie's desk, a combination electronic control center and sound studio which included two tape decks, an oscilloscope, hi-fi controls, editing equipment, and a typewriter...the UNIVERSE at a touch. From the desk Ernie could monitor all the happenings in the main house through an intricate intercom system, control his steambath, and the railroad turntable that sat in the driveway—not such an extravagance when one realizes that there were always many cars at the house, Ernie's or friends, with no place to turn around. Irving Manesfield, in a burst of goodwill, donated that to the cause one Christmas along with a copper-lined sauna. This monument was faced in one corner by a three-foot high inlaid Louis XIV type clock, perhaps a touch too ornate (not Edie's choice at all) but a fitting bauble, a good paperweight to boot.

Divided from the second and oldest level by a set of heavy darkwood planks with swords, points down, used as railing was the playroom which contained another fireplace, a bar, refrigerator, a small stove, a few more book cases, and a beautifully inlaid green felt cardtable with recessed pockets, Edie's gift. Naturally enough, over in a corner behind the poker table was a full suit of armor left over from the New York collection. Nothing at all like the old days in Philadelphia, no more need for front doors and drafts. To complete the obvious, not only was there a bathroom, but off that was Manesfield's sauna in which Ernie would host occasional steambath cardgames and some production meetings. No wonder production meetings were such a gas at the house.

Built into, or on top of that was a smaller loft space where Ernie stored his files, golf clubs, and spare ornaments. The perfect universe in all—the Pack or anybody else who came felt instantaneously at home in this Kovacs vision of the male environment. No one needed encouragement when Ernie told them to feel free. For the Pack it was possibly the ultimate hangout, but for one of Ernie's close friends, panelist Hans Conreid, it seemed to be "a grown-up little boy's room"—a description to which even Ernie, after some reflection, agreed.

Whatever way it seemed, the den definitively embodied the Kovacs ideal of togetherness. He believed in togetherness, up to a point...

However, what I think is BAD about togetherness, is this current business of HIS and HERS matching shirts, bathing suits and hockey sticks. Nothing makes me feel quite as foolish as even the coincidental wearing of the same colors in clothing, let alone a PURPOSEFUL wearing of the identical things. For instance, when my wife and I are both wearing our pokadot bathing suits (even though she looks better in a bathing suit than I do), I always feel we look like misguided twins who in some sort of confusion got married...Going on with this, beyond wearing purple slacks when I am wearing them, I ALSO do not want my wife smoking cigars, drinking boilermakers or playing poker all night. These things are MINE and MINE alone and the enjoyable aspects of all three of them is the fact that I am the ONLY one in the family participating in any of these rather enjoyable diversions.

In the male-dominated world which Ernie hosted, Edie stayed discretely in the background and enjoyed the informality. She complimented her husband perfectly as Edd Henry succinctly remarked, "Edie always had a bit of dignity and she always wanted to be at least the one that was the real hostess when you came to the house...she was very proper, she would dress, she was gracious, she wanted to be sure that you had whatever you needed either in food or in drink. Ernie naturally accepted the elegance she brought to his house, 'Relax and enjoy it, I'm here' he used to say, 'what else do you need?'"

According to Henry, the main ingredient of the Kovacs household was informal elegance, Edie provided the key, "All his simpleness was rubbing off on her but she maintained that air of elegance. When you came to the house of the hostess that Ernie took for granted, and you took it for granted because it was so elegant...everything was elegant with him. I think that was his life."

Elegance or Edie? Or a bit of both. She'd made the best of the situation, having given up a promising career to come west to be the attractive hostess—and if anyone was overshadowed in Hollywood it was Edie Adams, now Mrs. Ernie Kovacs, stepmother. She became an even better mother taking upon herself the responsibility for his children's education. Not only did she persuade Ernie to join a church, but she enrolled the children in Sunday School. In deference to her, Ernie built Edie a practice room, a music room, and over the garage an elegant sewing room where she worked on all her children's clothes as well as her own. Whenever Ernie went on location he always brought along his family, making it doubly difficult for any sort of career to mature, and when Edie did go on the road herself Ernie was uneasy.

Kippie and Bette thrived in the rich atmosphere of Hollywood and Ernie's success—they idolized their papa. Bette was so much of a fan that she learned all of his routines; friends said she was a chip off the old korner herself. Now that his life was complete, Ernie spoiled his children in typical fashion—each had her own wing in the house complete with television sets, telephones, and hi-fi's. Even their special slide which lead from their windows to the backyard pool. Animals of all descriptions found their way into the house, turtles, cats, dogs, though Ernie's special friend was a burro which sometimes kept him company in the den. Occasionally the animal would go on a rampage and eat a few scripts, but that was part of the fun—nothing like a dispassionate editor on-call at all hours.

Together they were a family as far as it was possible to be a family given Ern's work schedule and his daily habits. Perforce Edie not Ernie always made plans for weekend trips with the girls and planned Sunday, weeks in advance for Ernie was into Hollywood with a vengeance.

Not only was Hollywood the movie capitol of the day but also one of the higher roller centers of action—Vegas and Tahoe were short hops. Any game was fine with the olive just so long as he could lose. Long before Hollywood, gambling was an obsession bordering on mania but now with his Dom Perignon tastes he was beginning to learn how ruinous it could be. He may have been able to beat his cronies in New York to death with money, but here they all had money themselves—they could match him and raise him and even lose and they'd always have more. Funny money, Hollywood money—when when you're hot, you're hot, when you're not you owe and owe and owe.

No place for a gambling man's illusions. In those funzie games in the den where time froze and the Daniels flowed 'til dawn, Ernie was taken more than a few times by 'friends' who when not acting were professional cardplayers. Even as friends are friends, invariably in Hollywood or Vegas or wherever he chose to try his questionable luck, a mark is a mark...god knows Ernie was the archetypal mark. He couldn't have asked for a better profession than acting where the most predominant game is on-set gin...almost as good as a cigar tree, or as bad as a government lien on your life. He played it broad, there was nothing more he could do as gambling overtook his art, a lethal prop so much a part of character.

Actually one of the reasons Arnel and Manesfield hired Milt Hoffman in the first place was to try to stop Kovacs from playing cards on the set when the crews were ready. He was always asking, with Shear of course in his dressing room, "One more hand, one more hand" while the budget was shot to hell. Cards were so much a part of his routine that when he first met Hoffman he didn't ask him "Are you a good director?" or even "Where did you work last?" but "Do you play cards?" When Hoffman replied in the negative, he was almost fired before he was hired.

At that time Shear (it was thought) was the principle villain because Ernie always played with him (hell they'd been doing it for years, screw the rules, it's a good honest game, so what?) But when Shear was canned and Joe Behar was in charge Ernie found other takers, "I never played cards when I was working because that would really be defeating the whole idea," said Behar, "my idea was to get them out in the studio." Couldn't get the crew to say anything, they were making triple golden time.

Behar wasn't the only one who was annoyed. Many times Edie would get dressed to go out for the night with Ernie only to find him in the den in his shirtsleeves still at cards, "One more hand, one more hand" and she was getting no overtime, she was his wife.

When Irving Manesfield came west while TAGL was still his show, he and Ernie used to drive around and bet on license plates—odds or evens, first car on the left side far corner of La Cienega and Santa Monica...25 bucks says it's even. They kept their accounts in flux, though Manesfield used to get frantic late night calls from Ernie for small salary advances to pay creditors or some urgent gambling debt. He would get petulant when he couldn't have his way.

When Ernie and Edie played Vegas for the periodic supper club shot, more than one hotel management prohibited him from going near the tables for fear that he'd wind up losing his whole week's salary in a night. When he couldn't play he'd sometimes slip some money out of his vest to a friend to bet like the grown-up little boy he was all the while.

According to legend, while in Havana shooting a movie, Ernie one evening decided to make a long distance phone call to the States. The phone booth was fifteen feet from the crap tables; when he got a busy signal he went to the tables to kill some time and wound up losing a few hundred dollars. Of course he didn't need cards to lose money, there were far more interesting, novel ways to do it. While returning from Europe on a transatlantic liner, he once called up poor Irving in the middle of the night.

"Gotta deck of cards handy, Irving?"

Yeah said Manesfield groggily.

"OK," said Ernie, "$500 says that the first card you cut from the middle is red."

Silence...

"OK, double your money...another $500 says it's black."

Silence...click. Two weeks later Ernie had a check for the full amount.

Other times he wasn't as lucky when it came to collecting his own debts. There is one story told by Shear which seems characteristic. Once Ernie on a return trip to the Coast with a big Hollywood producer, lost $8,000 in a gin game; Ernie wrote the man a check on the spot. Two weeks later up in the den, the same producer dropped four or five grand to Ernie and then pleaded poverty, "I'm a little short right now," the man said, "I'll give you a check for a thousand." Forget it. "What are ya...crazy," said Shear who saw it all. "No, I don't want to do that," replied Ernie evenly.

With closer associates it was all on account to be totalled up sometime later on. At the studio he gambled for matches, split twenty dollars, whole, ten dollars, while in the den it was chips. These games were not the exclusive property of his more 'famous' cronies either—anyone could play...if they dared. When crew members dropped up for production meetings or whatever, Ernie always invited them to try their luck. Many declined because of the money on the table while those who joined were flabbergasted with poker a la Kovacs. Gene Lukowsky, Ernie's TD, more or less played regularly when his budget allowed. One evening he played cards from nine at night to three in the morning, "I was over my head and I had my checkbook with me," he recalled, "and I figured, well, I can go a couple of hundred dollars. We're playing with chips, no cash involved, and it turned out Milt Hoffman owed me about a hundred and a half, I owed Ernie about two bills, like that. And when we broke up, it was all for funzies...nobody paid anything. I thought if I had known—I was really playing them right to the vest and unless I had a cinch I wouldn't open or stay in the pot because you knew that was pretty big money for me. But if I had known it was all funzies, hell, I would have enjoyed the game a lot more. Nobody ever paid anybody else off." Funny, Hoffman said he didn't play cards, but guess that meant on the set. Maybe he liked hanging out, maybe he was used to cigars by then...maybe Ernie just suckered him into the game.

Kovacs was pretty easy to deal with (and to), though at the time of his death there were rumors that he owed a hell of a lot from those 'funzie' games. "He may have had a lot of IOU's out," said Marvin Moss who was playing more and more gin with his client as time wore on, "but I never really knew him to hold up on the loot. I must say with me he said, 'I'll give you a check tomorrow'. The worst it would be two days from tomorrow. I never had to chase him for money, maybe there were guys who did. I didn't...I didn't know anybody who did." There were also rumors that Ernie was in heavy debt to high rollers in both Vegas and Miami, though they evidently never wanted the publicity...and they could afford the dubious goodwill of having Kovacs in their debt.

Not that Ern cared whether he won or lost, he just enjoyed playing cards in any form, though enthusiasm counts for less when it comes to big money. He would even win big; at a post shower game for Jeannie Martin, Dean's fourth wife, Kovacs took a pot worth

$48,000 which must have surprised the hell out of players like Dean Martin who could make good money that way. Cards in any form were simply a part of his nature. The first question he'd ask was whether you smoked cigars, the second whether you played cards...care to try one...how about a few hands? Edd Henry summed it up decorously enough, "He was a high roller...he was a hard player. He played gin with love and determination, very serious about it all. He considered himself a champ (*but he used to lose a lot*-ed.) Oh he as a big loser, he was a challenger. He considered himself the best, and he wasn't because obviously he wouldn't be losing a lot if he was the best."

Part of the routine, the big cardplayer riverboat gambler with the big cigar. As an extended joke, Ernie hastily compiled a book for Doubleday in 1961 called, "How to Talk at Gin." Composed on dictabelts and based on conversations and conduct of people who played with him, "How to Talk at Gin" was profusely illustrated by the author "in a burst of self-confidence". It contained a kibitzer's deathless wisdom too true. Under the heading "Speed of Play, Quitting the Game, and Alibis" was the following notation:

> The slow player is a positive component of every gin group.
> There are three reasons for his being a slow player:
> 1. caution
> 2. cunning
> 3. stupidity

In the back he listed all his friends under various headings, great players, good players, and average players. His name was the only one in the 'great' category...natch.

A card is only a card in the hands of a professional, for a comedian it's a prop: Colloquoy between a journalist and a cigar-smoker after the journalist has asked whether he's doing anything after the day's shooting...eating maybe?

"Then you don't play," said Mr. Kovacs unhappily.

"Play what?"

"Poker," answered Mr. Kovacs with some derision. He added, "...a poker player knows that when he's asked what he's doing at night it means really how about a game of poker tonight?"

"I'm still available," replied the journalist.

"No, I'd feel too much like a shill if I got you into a game. If you lost you'd think I'd been trying to hook you. Knowing this, I would lose consciously (!!!), so there would be no point to the game. The trick is to get people to think the game is their idea."

Instead of writing about gin, Ernie should have written an opus called "A Hustler's Guide to Poker".

Where was it all going, all this money? Anybody's guess. The government was particularly interested in the Kovacs finances, they'd been after him since 1955 when he neglected paying his taxes while searching for his daughters. Part of the public Kovacs philosophy of finance—I made it, it's mine—though seriously Ernie was something less of a comedian on the subject. When asked by Marie Torre, a television columnist for the late lamented New York *Herald-Tribune,* "Tax is a word that causes a chill to people in show business—the tax structure has made it impossible for any one to get excited about financial reward for creative ability. It has become necessary for the financially short-lived to incorporate to legalize his keeping a few more bucks. It's rather discouraging to realize that when the smoke blows away from the gold print on the corporate door, the professional people of today really have no desire for all these business ramifications as such. They are merely trying to hold on to some of the original money they made as boxers, actors, and singers." Hardly lines from the life of the party, the center of entertainment for the Hollywood wrecking crew.

The government hounded him incessantly nonetheless and commenced garnishing his salaries in 1959, "It was the first time that I'd ever seen Ernie really worried about it because he realized that there was no way out of it" said Shear. "He was doing everything and anything: fish market openings, anything to get money to pay for the tax. He was grossing $800,000 a year, but I doubt if he was keeping a hundred—he kept going back into hock." Less funny when the government attached $90,000 of Ernie's $100,000 fee for making *Sail a Crooked Ship,* took it early and left the rest for the next time.

Lemmon offered him the services of his own business manager, but after four weeks, the manager gave up. "Ernie had nine corporations and then he'd go to Canada to get a few more called (sic) THE BAZOOKA DOOPA HIKKA HOOKA HOCKA COMPANY," said Lemmon enthusiastically, "...and crossing (over)—he was a brilliant sonofabitch. He had it so screwed up (that) they (IRS) couldn't figure anything out so they started attaching everything. They said, 'None of this can work, we can't understand.'"

Edie was more in the dark about Ernie's finances. He thought she had no business knowing about such mundane matters. She caught on soon enough, "...and the one thing that really got me was finally I had to take any job that was offered to me at any price and he (Ernie) thought, 'Where are you going, what's this crap?' He didn't understand it and I didn't understand it either." While they were forcing Ernie to make pictures he didn't need, they were applying pressure to Edie "...the last goodie was to do the "Today" Show in New York and fly back and forth on weekends...I was supposed to do it, I had to do it. I mean they offered it to me, they could have offered it to me for $500 a week." Fortunately no network is that cheap, even NBC.

Ernie fought as well as he was able, though by 1961 the taxboys were almost ready to tag his furniture to raise the cash. In a desperation move to buy time, Ernie signed away twenty thousand dollars in government bonds he'd been saving for the children. No jokes now, a deadly serious business of dollars and sense.

By mid-1961, there seemed to be a way out, for Ernie had finally found a business manager who could deal with his holding companies and could offer some sound financial advice. In July on the day the papers announced a $75,000 Income tax lien, Ernie announced the acquisition of the $2,000,000 California Racquet Club on a lease-back basis with the owner. When Edie heard the news over the phone, she reportedly told her husband, "Ernie, please try not to buy anything else until I get back." ...some joke.

Aside from movie money, Ernie had been trying other ploys to get himself out of hock; publishing seemed another possible source of income and he bombarded his editor Ken McCormick from Doubleday with an assortment of quickie book schemes. *Zoomar* had already sold 17,500 copies in the Doubleday printing by January, 1958. Kovacs actually was something of a minor literary light anyway. In April, 1959, he started another shorter book "John Has Fungas", a much more personal book which cross cut between his life at home and dissertations on the art of TV parody. (John, incidentally was the name of Kippie's pet turtle who'd developed a furry growth). No dice. In June of 1960, he enthusiastically hyped his editor on a book of his own pen and ink drawings and though McCormick thought they were pretty, he again regretfully passed them up.

Ernie's next book proposal in December '60 was a compendium of the wit and wisdom of Percy Dovetonsils, "I think the book should sell awfully well," he hopefully wrote, "for these reasons: over the past eight or ten years or more actually, Percy Dovetonsils has appeared coast-to-coast. The mail requesting a single copy of one poem ran as high as 5,000 a week, at one time. After all these years there are still frequent requests each week for a picture of Percy and/or a copy of the poem he ran." Again a regretful 'no' from New York who thought Percy came off on TV, though in book form he was less amusing.

Undaunted, Ernie commenced a far more ambitious project, a novel *Mildred Szabo,* set in Europe during World War I. The research alone required that he read many old papers and magazines of the period. But it was so bulky to transport that eventually a few hundred pages of the manuscript were lost somewhere in transit and the project was shelved.

Though he kept getting turndowns for his quickie books he corresponded regularly with his editor in New York. In the Fall of 1960, after the demise of TAGL, before the Specials he told McCormick, "I have been extremely busy since having left home and have been shooting every morning and returning at seven at night (in London). The days have all been twelve-hour ones and while I am now only working five days a week in London, while we were on location for some three and a half weeks, we were working seven days a week." More than busy, "I have another picture which I will do in June in Venice (*Five Golden Hours*). I think there is a possibility of one preceeding that in April, which would be done in Sicily. When I get home there will will be by then a completed script waiting for me to read on a picture to be shot in January ('61) in the States. The January picture will not take as much of my time as the two pictures abroad, the latter being leads. The one in the States is one of three leads with Jack Lemmon and Debbie Reynolds as the other two. Quite honestly I am not too anxious to do the one in the States as now I have done this picture with the main role." Business was, of course, business, "It might not be a good business tactic to do lesser roles for a while. However, I am under contract to Columbia and do not have script approval as the contract is some four years old."

Further on in the October, '60 letter, Ernie talked about his Specials in characteristic haste, "When I reach home the first thing I will have to do is to finish up quickly four or five half-hour television shows so that I can tape them to leave again in the Spring (1961)." The Specials were squeezed in among Ernie's other professional committments; by the time he shot six out of eight by the Summer of '61, his breathless energy appeared to be on the wane, "I tape them on weekends and am done up until December now. I just finished one yesterday (Aug. 30, 1961) and the taping sessions knock me

out...I have been directing them from the control room, and the first four were done on twenty-four hour stretches...now they're more complicated and I do them on Saturdays and Sundays...from six a.m. to four a.m. both days--"
(memo from Scott Runge, ABC Network Production Coordinator to Sandy Cummings re: Special #3...typical

> Everything short of turning off the power was done by Marvin Moss, Milt Hoffman and myself to have Ernie carry over to next Sunday, June 4th.
>
> My memo asking for a two Sunday taping as such was tossed out due to Ernie's shooting schedule and acceptable only if we were to go past eleven. My suggestion on splitting the crews were not found acceptable. My efforts and the efforts of others to wind it (up) earlier Sunday night and carry over to next Sunday, June 4th went down the drain. Everything possible was done to shut down, (and) carry over to June 4th date for taping and editing.

--"Mondays and Tuesdays are kind of washouts for me as I have miserable headaches from sitting in that more or less airless room." So Milt Hoffman wasn't just complainin' it appears.

There were also pressures which he brought on himself. With Ernie now the packager, or more accurately E&EK Productions, Dutch Masters was giving Ernie the full price as per budget each time he delivered a completed show. ABC would then re-bill for their below-the-line costs, studio time, camera rental, special effects, etc. Of course Kovacs was blowing his budget all to hell. Not that it was important right then that he was getting behind. More like a Mexican stand-off with the studio, any studio's dealings with any packager, summed up succinctly by one old Hollywood hand, "Studio's always fuck you." If you watched them all the time, maybe not, but an agent can only do so much against indices of time and space.

They battled, agent and studio, in the grey, in the area of ferinstance: ferinstance when a director can't get a shot, it's the director's fault, hence the packager pays. When a studio camera blows out and time's wasted finding a replacement, then the studio's at fault...very simple...very not so simple.

THE SYSTEM which most alert agents had worked out to deal with the obvious was curious in its simplicity...hold them up, hold them up in the face of threats, in the face of pleadings...let 'em wait while:

--letter from Milt Hoffman to Ned Tanen (MCA) re: Special #2

Enclosed you will find the final 'below-the-line' billing for the Ernie Kovacs Special #1.
I have informed John Wagner who is the comptroller for the West Coast that E and EK Enterprises Inc. refuses to pay the penalties for production and engineering crews for the reasons outlined in my letter...
They were as follows:
1. failure of kaleidescope which necessitated re-shooting a replacement sequence.
2. improper information as to BAC's abilities to mat correctly.
3. failure of the makeup department to follow the makeup instructions as outlined by Mr. Kovacs in the production meeting.
4. the long stage waits included the injury to ABC personnel which alone held up shooting for an hour and fifteen minutes.
5. the errors in the pre-show estimates in regard to carpenter, show onset and carpenter show construction.

--letter from Milt Hoffman to Marvin Moss

Enclosed please find correct billing for No. 2 Kovacs

Special. As you see, this show was very heavy in construction and special effects. However, if we do not pay the engineering penalties and production penalties, we can pull back $5,378.80, leaving a very disrespectful total of $29,556.40. I have checked this bill over and over looking for a way out, but unfortunately for us ABC made no goofs.

etc..etc..etc.....

Delay and obstruct, scream your agent's lungs out, "...and then I go in and find the obvious things where they fucked him and started screaming. I'm not saying that all those things were false...I used to pick up odd things and go screaming about it whenever I found one, then I'd hold up the bills...paying them. When they'd really start screaming for the money, I'd go to them and say, 'Look I really don't have the time, but I found this, I found this...$65 dollars. (they'd say) 'we'll take it off the bill' and I'd start to argue, 'Take the 5 percent off or 10 percent off the whole bill, and I'll give you a check right now.'" Marvin was only trying to help his client, "...it was his money anyway, it didn't mean anything to me. I'm trying to help him, and that's what I used to do."

When Ernie himself was asked about the bind, he still maintained a surface bravado, AP style, "I'll tell you why I'm a nut, I'm a nut because I'm working for nothing. Take this television show I'm putting together. The network gives me $40,000 to produce a half hour of entertainment and it is costing me $50,000 or more. Even with a tremendous turnover and volume I've got to lose money. If I keep this up, I'll go into bankruptcy. I'm writing, directing, producing, and starring in four of these shows, but I can't afford to pay myself salaries." Ernie and the network had deducted their costs from the total package and given Ernie the difference. When they finally got around to demanding their costs they found to their dismay that the olive had already spent the money elsewhere.

As 1961 drew to a close, the pressure was becoming unbearable. In the midst of feverish studio activity Ernie would throw up his hands in disgust, depressed beyond measure, "I'll never get out of this" he told anyone who would listen, Milt Hoffman or Joe Behar during those long post-taping sweetening sessions in the editing room. He was pushing himself beyond his own limits.

Ernie Kovacs was in danger of being another statistic in the land of tinsel dreams but he had to show THEM he was good enough. He continued to hold out his own kinds of carrots to maintain his sanity, and while working he was hustling more books for Doubleday. In the Fall of 1961, he again wrote his editor Ken McCormick about new projects:

> I will be doing a pilot for a 'series' ...if it sells, I will be spending most of my days there and they are going to fix me up with a trailer-office so that I can work for Doubleday on the side."

and more money, an advance for his new book *Please Excusa Da Pencil,* slated to appear in 1962, "It is possible that I may have to secure some income before the end of the year or my deductions aren't going to hold up. If so, might we set *Please Excusa Da Pencil* for '61 sale with as large an advance as humanly possible?"

Working himself into the ground and playing cards to make up for working with equal intensity, Kovacs was overreaching himself. Friends were worried. A few days before his death in January, 1962, Ernie went to Dominic's to see Jack Lemmon and his wife Felicia for a drink. Lemmon noticed he was tired, "...he was taping some shows and there was something in his eyes...very, very, strange and I remember." He remarked to his wife when Ernie had gone, "I'm terribly worried about Ernie, I really think that something terrible is going to happen." A feeling; two days later the phone rang.

At the last gasp Ernie was beginning to see some relief. He was beginning to get some new tax advice from a new business manager who was straightening out the last ten years of financial chaos. After taping his last special he was planning to go to New York with his

Edie who was going back to Broadway in February, while he was toying with the idea of directing a straight play sometime in February as well. In the Fall he was slated to direct a Broadway musical called *Izzie and Moe*. He was also negotiating a production deal for five movies with Alex Guiness with whom he'd become good friends after they both worked in *Our Man in Havana*. THEY'D see eventually, and even if it wasn't in Hollywood, THEY'D find out soon enough.

Dutch Masters was also after Ernie to allow them to run some of his silent commercials independently of the show since they were such classics and the viewer response was overwhelming. Those residuals were looking better and better. Two days before the end, Milt Hoffman and Ernie were beginning work on some story boards for silent commercials for Colgate-Palmolive, just received a check for development, another sure money winner. He wasn't too enthusiastic about that kind of commercial success, but he knew he needed the money—whatthehell.

January 13, 1962, started normally enough for Ernie Kovacs—bed after a late night poker session, possibly a steambath or another bout with the becoming *Mildred Szabo.* He was up bright and early, hopped in his vintage white Rolls, and was off to Griffith Park for another day on the set of *A Pony for Chris,* playing a variation on his familiar Hollywood role, a snakeoil salesman in the old west aided by his silent Indian sidekick Buster Keaton. At about six or six-thirty he drove over to the ABC television studios on Prospect Avenue off Hollywood Boulevard in Los Feliz to work on a sweetening session with Gene Lukowsky, where music was added and the sharp transitions between the taped bits ironed out. By 10 he was finished and off again with a long night still ahead.

Later on that evening he was to meet Edie at a Christening party for Milton Berle's son Michael held at Billy Wilder's house, though he still had time for a drink with his cardplaying hustler friend Joe Miklas at PJ's. After a suitable interval he proceeded on to Wilder's, pushing that heavy car down Santa Monica Blvd. toward Wilshire.

It was amazing that Ernie drove at all, considering his own feelings. Whenever possible he preferred to be driven, chauffeur or friend. Not the greatest driver by any stretch of the imagination, not wanting to be by this time...such a bore...all you need a car for is to get from one place to the other, no need to get flashy. No, Ernie had passed through that love affair with car and speed though he was always mildly amused by his cronies' excess zeal in the pursuit of the ultimate machine. One time his friend Lemmon got an Aus-tin-Martin as part of his hi-jinks income stretching act. A few weeks later the head cracked—Ernie thought that was funnier than hell...poetic justice, tryin' to get flashy, eh Jack...pow!

Wilder's party wasn't spectacular—old friends, a tribal gathering. Edie had come down from the house with the new white Corvair stationwagon. At Wilder's were many of his Hollywood 'friends' those with whom he played cards, those who enjoyed his special humor, even some close friends who besides Wilder, included Lemmon and Quine as well as Lucille Ball and her new husband, Gary Morton, Berle and wife, Yves Montand. No press agents (unless as friends), no starlets...

Recurring flashes of familiar faces AND Ernie, the kid from Trenton with all these names, those he'd lampooned so many years before. "Hi, Ern, how's the pilot working out?" ..."Your newest picture should be a gas" ..."Now what Ern, where's the game tonight?"

"Not tonight fellas" or "Yeah, everything's going fine," then launching into an account of the day's events in vivid detail. It must have been increasingly more difficult for Ernie to live with his own demons while knowing that he was better, more talented. THEY were making the money, looking at their contented Hollywoodized personalities, all that showbiz behind them and look how calm and self-assured they are...and me, what the fuck am I doing, why can't I get a chance, what's the use of knowing Wilder if he won't let me do something great, yet he comes to my house, why, why? Some movie contract, this--

> Look Ernie, you're not top box office material, you've got a mustache and you look too ethnic for those dramatic roles. Stick with these parts and at least you'll work...you'll have work as long as you live. You'll have parts as long as you live...

Aw stuff it, willya, man, go peddle your agency flesh--

Being under all that hair and cigar smoke essentially a shy man, Ernie overcompensated among his immediate 'peers', reverting to type----the life of the party, miles and miles away from his den, his kingdom:

Item from AP story, *Philadelphia Enquirer,* Jan. 13, 1962:

> Comedian Gary Morton who attended the baby shower with his recent bride, Lucille Ball, recalled: "Ernie was in great form at the party. He had just finished this western pilot and was in high spirits. He described vividly and with great wit and humor—his experiences."
>
> The Kovacs cigar was in great evidence.
>
> Ernie told how cold it was on location for the pilot film and recounted—as only he could—his experiences when they told him to take his shirt off.
>
> He rocked us with laughter describing how shivery he was.
>
> It was, of course, a very warm occasion, and Ernie added the warmth that only he could add.

For Kovacs it was the same old movie in the land of movie shades in costume and prop—life of the party, being himself, or whatever approximation he manifested, with his 'friends' of five-years standing. Five years and he still had a case of the syndrome. Eugene is script-city without a script—his 'friends' had the monopoly. Popular in the popular eye...be damned—at least he wrote his own material which is more than he could say for Berle—jeez.

Wilder and Lemmon understood, but what could they do? They were successful in spite of the system and I'm the misfit, the accepted misfit, the kook...

Living in Hollywood was like being one step from Forest Lawn with a press release funeral in the background, vistas of aimless wandering between Dominic's, PJ's, or the Villa Capri. Ernie Kovacs had sworn off gambling again by January, 1962:

Edie and I returned to Vegas this morning...This is a town I really loathe...I don't gamble there anymore and I still loathe it.

letter to McCormick

Hollywood had become the dead end; the pot of gold contained taxmen and their clipboards...fuck 'em, I earned the money, I'll keep it, just see if you can get your fucking hands on it you bastards...so, I'll sign over the bonds (get some time to figger a way to stop them)...

...but THEY come to me in the den, my den, they all come and we have a great time shooting the shit and playing cards and there's no one around to bother us (er...me). Maybe I'll finish Mildred Szabo and sell it to Ken for some BUCKS, need some BUCKS, need some real work...anything. OK, I'll go to New York and take that play, whatever in hell it is, make it into something, the ole Kovacs touch. Also I'll keep an eye on Edie, keep those men from slobbering all over her—fucking Edie...Jeez what am I gonna do about this fucking mess...

This party's a goddamn tape loop...Howareya Milton, congrats. Here's something for the kid...hope he'll use it well...hope you can keep up the payments—boy!

A party like in Trenton when you put the lights out, switch, only here they write press releases...vision of the reality of the dream—the Rat Pack...jeez with agent variations:

Ernie tried to get into the Hollywood scene, it was important to him. And he was socially accepted by the group that was active at the time...The Rat Pack, the Wilders, the whole thing being invited to those parties and so forth...and he was invited he did get to meet those people and they did like him.

Yes Marvin, pray continue, the vision...Ernie in Kovacsland?...hardly:

Jean Martin gave a baby shower at her house, and Ernie was—if the Rat Pack existed—Ernie was, if not in it, on the edge he was close to it, he wasn't really in it I would say, but he was close to it—

sez E: Outside of a brief association I once had with a fraternal organization (which I joined mostly because they had slot-machines in back) I have always had an antipathy to organizations. The members of the Rat Pack are, individually, good friends of mine and Edie's. However, nothing would embarass me more, personally, to think I was a member of a little group. This would eventually lead to our all wearing identical beanies with "Rat Pack" on the front and a local tavern as sponsor on the back of our sweat shirts. I've never been much of an advocate of "Hey fellows, let's go in for a swim" type of existence and neither has Edie. I would hate to go into my old age greeting friends with a secret handshake.

...and Jeanie Martin gave this party and I was invited and that wasn't my regular group, and I was impressed I will admit...and I walk in and here standing around the bar is Dean, Frank, Milton Berle, Shirley MacLaine, and Lemmon...it could have been West Covina, I could tell you. Then it was dinner time, right to the buffet and we got our plates filled, sat down, had dinner, and after dinner, the ladies went into the den and opened the shower presents, and I went into the bar and Milton Berle got up and gave ten minutes of stale jokes, the worst, the same thing as the guy in West Covina who would have put a lampshade on his head, not better. Dean finally said, 'oh fuck this Milton' and they started a poker game—I wasn't about to get into that poker game and that was one of the dullest evenings I've ever spent in my whole life.

Like all the other parties, Ern was 'on' for his friends, on top of the Hollywood syndrome and in the game for keeps.   Ernie left the party at one o'clock after bidding adieu's; he was going back to PJ's for a nightcap with Miklas, then home for some work. Instead of the Rolls he took the Corvair, easier to maneuver in his condition. He never made it to PJ's or his den—ever again. Minutes after leaving Wilder's, Ernie wrapped himself around a pole at the intersection of Beverly Glen and Santa Monica Blvd., in a freak accident, fatigue overriding his reflexes in heavy metal crunch, instantaneous death ten days before his 43rd birthday.

After the gruesome truth was established by Lemmon, and funeral arrangements were made, Ernie was still our ironical soul, even in repose. As a favor to Edie, Lemmon went down to the funeral parlor to put some cigars in Ernie's pockets for a last sentimental gesture. Sequel to Eugene, much before the film of *The Loved One.* Lemmon in Kovacsland? "...but when I went down with the bloody cigars. It was so awful and bizarre because there he was, how they had dressed him all up, and this pimply-faced kid is there saying, 'We're *terribly* proud, we *really are* of the job we've done...I think he looks marvy...I assume it will be open?' and I said 'No, it's gonna be closed'. 'Oh' and he's just looking at Ernie and beaming at the work that he has done. Now I go to put the cigars in (but) I can't open it up (the pocket). It's tight, the clothes are form fitting. He's got it pulled in the back and everything else, and I'm trying to get the cigars in the pocket and I'm thinking, 'Holy Jesus and now they're flaking all over the place.' Now this guy (the pimply faced attendant) is going beserk. It was so bizarre and awful, and then I started to laugh because what else can you do? I said, 'I can't believe this is happening. (*Like a bit he would do?*-ed) Exactly, that's why I'm laughing, precisely, I said I might have known it would happen with that now 'cause I know he was circling overhead and laughing his ass off."

Ernie's funeral was a Hollywood event of rare import, many stars Ernie knew personally and many he didn't know, that Edie thought should come, did to pay tribute. The agents oversaw the invited guests at the church of which Ernie was nominally a member, just a few blocks from the scene of the accident. The regular minister was out of town and his assistant was called on for eulogy. Edie thought that would save needless bickering among his friends. He read an Edgar A. Guest poem called "Somebody Said It Couldn't Be Done", a saccarine piece of doggerel, "...for Ernie Kovacs, one of the most original, bright writers and performers and directors that we have ever known. Now I want to tell you, if Ernie wasn't buzzing overhead up there in hysterics, there's no way he wasn't," said Lemmon. Percy Dovetonsils maybe, not Edgar Guest. Whatta finale, carried to the final reward by Lemmon, Sinatra, Joe Miklas, Dean Martin, and Ernie's brother, Tom. Crowds of the famous— Edward G. Robinson, George Burns, Benny, Kim Novak, Danny Thomas, Sam Goldwyn, Jimmy Stewart...all of them were there, for they respected his shade.

Joe Behar, Ernie's first director was there with the famous and caught the irony of it all, "Those funerals, those funerals at those things, I've never been a funeral celebrity and you go there and it's so funny. They got two agents from MCA who stand at the front door and make sure that everybody who goes in there knew him, who wasn't just gate crashing, but it's so funny to see two agents, two sharpies from MCA standing there kind of screening everybody as they went in. It's almost like when he was alive and they did that and after he's dead they're still representing him."

Tell 'em Marvin: "I remember at the funeral there was me, I think Joe Miklas, and somebody else who we figured between the three of us knew everybody that Ernie knew, and we stood by the door of the church like to decide who would get in and who wouldn't. We knew everybody...but it wasn't a scene at the church, it was very interesting. At the church a lot of tourists showed up but they stayed outside, they didn't try to get in."

Even dying didn't extricate Kovacs from his financial problems, and the days, weeks, months, and years afterwards were almost nightmarish ones for Edie, Kippie, Bette, and Mia Susan born in 1959. Ernie's death released a torrent of condolences not only from people in the immediate community but in newspaper reporters and radio journalists throughout the country. The press agents had a difficult time screening the sympathetic from the ghoulish curiosity seekers. Weeks afterward, the second wave hit. At the time of his death, Ernie's estate was valued at well over two million dollars, though there was approximately $7,000 in ready assets as opposed to claims of well over $150,000, before Ernie's shadows, the Internal Revenue Service had their shot. Beside claims to $71,628 for overdue payments in 1959, the IRS filed a second lien against the estate for an additional $130,165.47 for Ernie's failure to pay income tax in 1956-67...a cool $200,000.

Two and a half weeks after the accident, ABC also filed against the estate for $220,632 claiming that E&EK Productions failed to pay them for the accumulated 'below-the-line' costs of stage managers, technical directors, film editors, etc., though they were willing to settle for 7 percent of the total monies owed. ABC had really no thought of collecting the money, they merely wanted to establish tax credit to deduct the debt themselves—suing the estate assured their tax loss. THE SYSTEM was indeed wrecking its revenge, and no longer would Moss have to temporize with the studio.

Ernie's friends offered to do a benefit for Edie and her family but she graciously turned them down, even though she was now fighting for her life, her children's existence, and her house. Then the vultures descended. Ernie's first wife, Bette came from Florida to lay claim to both Ernie's estate as his legal wife (Mexican marriage was contested) and mother of Kippie and Bette. After a messy and quite sensationalist public hearing and trial, her claim was disallowed, and the children remained with their stepmother. A year later, Mary Kovacs, Ernie's outspoken mother who never really liked Edie anyway accused her of mismanaging Ernie's estate and being an unfit mother. She petitioned the courts for control of the assets and again the children. Ironically enough she had testified against Bette in the previous year's custody battle.

Mary also accused Edie of withholding monies due her from insurance policies Ernie supposedly took out in her name. However there was no policy for her and never had been. Undoubtedly he'd meant to but instead the insurance went to his children and was underwritten in such a manner that neither the government nor ABC could attach it for themselves. Mary went to court in 1966, and lost. He'd paid rent on her apartment on Hollywood Boulevard and provided her with a car, no more could he do. The pot at the end of the Hollywood rainbow was tapped out. Said Moss the stage manager in passing, "...the wife did come from Florida and she was looking for the loot—the kids and the attendant loot; Mary was looking for the loot that she was supposed to have...and there was no loot to have. People are like that, they all thought there was a lot of money there and there wasn't."

End of the dream and the epoch.

Ernie's death thrust his sheltered wife into the unwelcomed light of the most lurid publicity. Not only did she successfully defend her position as mother and executor of his legacy but she also subsequently prospered herself. Through her own diligent work and a few courses at UCLA, she mastered the intricacies of Ernie's tax debauch paying off all his outstanding debts and maintaining possession of his house. She lives there today in the company of her third husband, bandleader Pete Condoli and Mia Susan, her daughter. Kippie and Bette are pursuing their careers in theatre; Kippie has Ernie's white Rolls.

Today the den remains pretty much intact except for some spare armament which Edie put into storage. When you walk in and peer down to the third level you almost expect to see a billowing cloud of Havana cigar smoke from over the desk where the olive created...hi Ern.

It's
Been
Real

7

I've never had quite the same thing happen with other people, close friends, or my father or mother or other people very close like that passed away so far wherein the memory is so indelible that you forget sometimes that they're gone...a year or year and a half later they are still indelible in your mind and you still think about them. Several times I got caught literally and I couldn't believe myself...off guard months later I'd suddenly say when somebody was talking, "Oh shit, that's wonderful, wait until Ernie hears it..." I'd forget. He was still there because he was really such an individual and unique and definite personality. He really left a mark, he wasn't just a talented nice guy.

Jack Lemmon

I've never had quite the same thing happen with other people, close friends, or my father or mother or other people very close like that passed away so far wherein the memory is so indelible that you forget sometimes that they're gone...a year or year and a half later they are still indelible in your mind and you still think about them. Several times I got caught literally and I couldn't believe myself...off guard months later I'd suddenly say when somebody was talking, "Oh shit, that's wonderful, wait until Ernie hears it..." I'd forget. He was still there because he was really such an individual and unique and definite personality. He really left a mark, he wasn't just a talented nice guy.

Jack Lemmon

It still impresses me that you want to write the book because it just seems so hard for me to believe that other people feel the same way I do...he was really like my personal friend and nobody else had him as a friend, and yet I know the other guys had him as friends, but somehow he seemed special to us, he was our special friend.

Bob Kemp, ABC cameraman

After you worked with him you could work for years and they all looked like babies.

Barbara Murphy,
wardrobe mistress TAGL

I couldn't smoke the last cigar he gave me after he died. I just couldn't smoke it, it was a big Cuban thing. It finally died in the refrigerator, it just fell apart. I couldn't smoke it really, isn't that weird? I should have had a Jack Daniels and smoked it.

Bob Haley, ABC cameraman

It's been more than a decade since Ernie wrapped himself around a phone pole on Santa Monica Blvd., yet the boys on the back lot remember, be it ABC, Dumont (now WNEW), WTTM, WPTZ, CBS—he just hasn't been in the control booth lately. Those questionable comedic masterpieces run late into the night as Captain Segurra plays checkers with Wormwood using miniature whiskey bottles, getting smashed in timeloop eternally. College students can see "Kovacs," a documentary sponsored by the Dutch Masters Company compiled by Jack Mogulescu and Terry Gallany which contains bits from "Take a Good Look" and the Specials...two years out of a possible twelve. As for the rest, Dumont destroyed all their kinescopes during an economy drive a few years back. NBC has some salted away in a warehouse in New Jersey or upstate New York. It costs a fortune to track them down, much less to see them. CBS, WPTZ, and WTTM have snippets, while the audio portions of Ernie's shows from 1952-4 from Dumont and CBS reside in the Kovacs archives deep in the vaults of UCLA's special collections...over 200 lp's. And they still remember that fabulous shot.

One legendary party Ernie hosted for his ABC crew at the Villa Capri cost him $5,000. He came up to Bob Haley during the melee and deliriously exhorted him, "Hey Bob, go around and tell everybody to drink triple martinis, drink, drink the best Cognac. Go throw up, get sick, come back and drink more, get sick, drink more, that way word will get around Hollywood that not only do I drink but my friends drink too."

Haley organized a party for Ernie and Edie one Christmas by soliciting ten dollars from the crew—six or seven hundred dollars in all. Ernie had already been through the Pack, Wilder's and Lemmon's before he hit the Matador where Haley and the boys were holding forth. With tears in his eyes he exclaimed, "It's the best party I've been to in five days of partying." "--and it was a really neat party because the people that worked with him threw it," remarked Bob. "It's a rarity for that to happen in Hollywood. It *does* happen, Steve Allen throws a party once in a while, it does happen, I'm not saying it don't, but most of the time it don't, not when you're a technician."

"The parties were unbelievable," adds Kemp, "it was a first class arrangement, all first class. We've had a lot of parties around here but I guess his parties have been just about the best. The big parties were off the lot and they were for wives, husbands, boyfriends, girlfriends, whatever, and you could bring them, that was fine. They were invited. And if you brought a friend that was fine too. It wasn't like he was a big Hollywood star and you were sitting there at his party, we were just having a party." All that plus overtime and it wasn't even work.

"It didn't matter, it didn't matter what you did, you could be as creative as you wanted," reiterates Haley jovially, "Every week you looked forward to doing the show and after twenty-four hours you hated to go home. Now that's never happened in television...it's like a party, a total trip. Off camera, off set it was still a party. Comeon up to the house and play some cards anytime boys." "Yeah," said Kemp, "there was big money at the table, couldn't cut that, a lot of hundred dollar bills, stuff like that, a lot of gin, but I wasn't ready for that."

OK if not cards, how 'bout a drink? Ernie liked to give away bottles, just comeon up. "I used to go up to the house anytime I wanted to, I was welcome. I used to take some advantage of it...not too much. I didn't want to go there and drink all his wine, which I would have." Haley used to get a case of wine every so often with notes, "Here are six bottles, I want you to let me know what it's like,

and these six bottles, just enjoy." He sent me some great wine, just great. Is this Hollywood? Not according to Haley:

> It's really a coldshot...Kovacs never had to give anyone anything at Christmas. He's the only person I've met that never had to give anything on birthdays or whatever...because he gave them it all year...Every show, every show...if there were twenty people there there would be twenty-five or thirty or forty pizzas, large ones of different shapes, kinds, flavors plus rigatoni and chili from Chassen's. Cases of wine and beer plus anything else you could bloody well think of...it's yours.

The freewheeling spirit generated on set extended to practical jokes mostly at the expense of poor Percy, a perennial favorite of the Kovacs crews. Once back at NBC, Shear decided to slip Dovetonsils a mickey for everyone knew Ernie's habits. "We knew damn well he never had any breakfast," said Perry Cross, co-conspirator, "and he probably didn't have dinner, and he wrote all night." Percy, by established custom, was a tippler and when reading liked to have a deepdish martini handy for moral courage. One morning 2½ ounces of tequila was substituted. When Ernie gulped it down as per script he was literally smashed on the set, rooted to his chair. Partially putting on the guys and partly because he was really leveled, he sat in his armchair for the remainder of the show emitting tearful drunken umphs, tears streaming from beneath his crosseyed glasses. On another occasion someone put a goldfish within the same glass. Finally Ernie plotted revenge.

For whatever reasons, Ernie thought Perry was responsible for all the on-set nonsense. At that time Perry used to work the floor while Shear caught the angles in the booth. Coming back from a commercial after a superclod bit (Superclod being so weak that he couldn't open windows, etc.), Ernie disappeared. Barry yelled at Perry to get on camera quick, "Do Something!!" Cross confronted the perplexed studio audience lamely, "Ladies and Gentlemen, there seems to be something wrong," blah, blah, blahing on camera with no Ernie and no Edie—help!

Edie popped up from nowhere and announced, "This is our producer, a very talented man," and then the Archy Cody Trio struck up "Slippin' and a Slidin'," a rock and roll tune which Perry had mocked to Ernie some time ago. "Now the audience I'm sure didn't know what the hell was going on," he said, "but Ernie had this high-pitched laugh. I could hear him laughing down the hall. And they all just disappeared...that was it...I could have killed him."

Besides the famous ABC video substitution Percy, the boys at ABC pulled another switcheroo, Jack Daniels for gin. Percy pursed his lips, sipped and lisped, "Hm...who ever thought of brown gin?" "I almost fell off my camera," said Haley, "because what is a guy going to say?...there's no other way to explain why it's brown."

Ernie's humor was never for everyone, Pablo's magic lens into Kovacsland, seeing crewseye problems, their special friend...colloquy with the staff photographer:

Well his humor wasn't for everyone.
No, he was for himself, he really didn't care about the people at home. He was losing money on the show, I don't know financially how it really turned out but I think that every week he lost a lot of money...

...because of the sets he was building?
Yeah, and it cost 800 or a thousand, it didn't matter, the point was that it had to be a certain way.

That's the mark of an artist
Yes, it gets very expensive and sometimes you have to make a compromise, but Ernie wouldn't compromise...you see he was striving for his artistic point, he had to make that, it was terribly important to him, it didn't matter what the network thought, it didn't matter what the people at home thought, he had to do it his way...and he did it great.

Not great in the Trendex sense either. "The Kovacs show never had good ratings," said Moss. (They had a loyal bunch who watched?—ed.) "Fuck that, Ernie Kovacs sold Dutch Masters cigars, that was the ballgame, that's what Mogulescu cared about and rightfully so. He didn't give a shit what the rating was, sure he wanted to be number one in the ratings." Kovacs was an acquired taste anyway.

He bridled in his vision against the specious rationality of cost accountants and the twelve-year-old mentalities of the sponsors who were wasting a creative medium while executives temporized. At the time Robert Kitner, former president of NBC in the late Fifties saw some of the problem, "I think and, in fact, all the networks, have balanced programming which we know, for example, a great bulk of the people in this country do not particularly care for." Peter Leavathes, former president of 20th Century Fox television made a far blunter statement of condition, "You've got to look at television realistically, as what it is today (1960). The sponsor buys a show to sell his product. That is the basic purpose of tv. To sell someone's product. And to do that you've got to be entertaining...A sponsor doesn't care at least in most cases he doesn't, how you sell his wares.

Networks explained and explained to Congress, which at the time was investigating the rigging of the then popular Quiz shows "21" and "The $64,000 Question," learning how sponsors had coached children into cheating while the sales of Geritol boomed. That's entertainment? For whom, why the lady from Cincinnati of course, a woman who according to an unpublished Kovacs article for *Life,* "...makes a list of all the commercial products they (programs) sell, frantically switching back and forth among the three stations so as not to miss any of the commercial announcements which she prefers to guest stars and would object if they were cut down in time or volume." Because of this mythical creature, part housewife, part hooker, all programming was geared—a nasty turn of affairs in a new enlightening medium. He concludes with some reasoning, "If there is something to the conception of 'the woman from Cincinnati' then the clothing industry can simplify its production by manufacturing just one fabric and one design in the future, one size."

In the 1957 draft of the article he talked about the never-ending parade of misery billed as entertainment quiz shows. He had good reason for once telling Barbara Murphy, "Don't watch too much television because it will only clutter your mind"...true, too true.

He brought the vision to television, you had to look carefully for the nostril flair—his 'special friends' on the crew knew that instinctively: "He wanted people to sit, he was trying to educate on all his shows for the subtle quiet humor, the 'hah hah' instead of the 'hahahaha'. He wanted people to watch the screen at all times...you gotta watch it like in the movies," said Haley munching imaginery popcorn while expostulating, stuffing the whole box into his mouth, transfixed. Good old Eugene.

Wonder is a pie in the face, or the White Rock fairy taking a bath. Ernie loved his pies and on occasion got carried away—hell of a way to make a living, eh guys? During an NBC morning extravaganza production of "By the Sea," complete with gay nineties costumes and a pie vendor selling his wares, the spontaneous vision overtook the script. While Edie was thrushing, Ernie went to purchase a pie from vendor Wendell whose crooked pie arm met the Kovacs kisser. Wendell ducked Ernie's return shot and a meringue free-for-all commenced. One sent Edie sprawling into 15 inches of goo. Meanwhile Kovacs and Bill ran back to the lockers for more ammunition. Then Ernie, four pies on his broad arms turned to Bill—"I've got mine," he gleefully said. Hell of a way to make a living, right guys?

By the finale not only was the entire cast covered with pie but also the producer, the director, most of the cameramen, and the band. Ernie wound up paying for one trumpet and replacing the watch of one of the chorus members which he, of course, suitably inscribed.

Inscription was a big thing with Ernie anyway. He once got into hot water with a top executive from NBC for giving Shirley Mellner a credit on a Special. Assistants never get credit, said the executive from his molehill, everyone else will want one...besides it's against company rules. "But she's always gotten Associate or

Assistant Producer, that's her credit," Ernie said. The executive wasn't impressed. Kovacs was adamant...er pissed, "Well then, there'll be no credits." Shirl told him to forget it, the show was more important.

When the show was finally aired a few weeks later, Ernie as per usual gave a small party for the staff. Ernie gave Shirley a gold charm bracelet with a heart and a loving cup. Over the heart was engraved "Assistant Producer," and on the back of the loving cup "Screw Hal Kemp"...and that was for real.

Actually Ernie commemorated many occasions with style even if and when (shudder!) he had to admit he was wrong. When Milt Hoffman fired one of Ernie's staff, he was mad enough to try to have Hoffman canned. Eventually Hoffman proved himself right. Ernie woke him up at four in the morning to tell him so and then sent him a pair of gold cufflinks which were inscribed, "Where the fuck is...Peggy?"

As for language, Ernie swore with love and abandon which was accepted after a fashion. Hoffman once hired a secretary and the first time Ernie spied her he said, naturally enough (since he had a good eye for girls), "Baby, I'd like to fuck you," not that unreasonable a statement in Hollywood, land of the creamy thigh. The lady ran to Milt who explained, "If Ernie didn't like you he wouldn't be able to say that to you...and he only talks dirty to people he would like." No further problems.

Marianne Hooper, one of Ernie's production assistants at ABC, now a producer for NBC, recalled similar circumstances, "He was volatile. He used to cuss a lot in the booth and it was funny the first time I was there, but it was like part of his vocabulary...and when I was in the booth he turned around and said, 'Excuse me'. It was so much a part of him. Since I was new he wanted to make sure I wasn't offended—it just shows his sensitivity."

He could also be a frequent recipient of razzberries from his crews as per the rules of the road. "With Ernie it didn't matter what you said to him," said Kemp "(one day) I said, 'Fuck you Ernie,' I just got pissed off at him. I could say that to him, and it would go at that.

I couldn't think of saying that to Sinatra (with whom he worked), I don't know what would happen, but I just couldn't say *that,* it was always 'Mister Sinatra'." Go fuck yourself Ern...it's been real.

In an atmosphere free of rules, Kovacs and his boys created masterpieces—all one had to give was interest, love, and dedication. Let's see what you guys want...why not? you know your own camera:

> I've worked on two shows that were creative...Garroway and Kovacs. They were truly creative shows from my standpoint because I could do my expression with my camera...what you put down was yours. No one told me what to put down. Usually it's one or two cameramen who do the show, but in this case it was all the cameramen, three or four guys and me, some were a little more creative than others, and some couldn't add and some could, but it was all the same.
>
> Haley

The highpoint of everyone's career on the ABC lot was working for the olive:

> I've done 10,000 television shows on stage, a lot of shows...and I'll tell you that the Kovacs show gotta be one of the best, that and the Julie Andrews Show...I always think of the Kovacs show as being one of the best. I've got a big picture of Ernie, a 16x20 of Percy Dovetonsils in my study and I just enjoyed looking at it. I also have a letter that Ernie sent me which says something like 'Thanks' and the Emmy we got for the show which is great, and yet the Emmy doesn't mean as much to me on the Ernie Kovacs Show as it does for the Julie Andrews Show. The Julie Andrews Show I did and I worked for it and I

created what I hope got me the Emmy, but on the Kovacs Show Ernie did it, Ernie created this monstrosity that turned out to be an artistic great thing that people loved and we won the Emmy for it which was beautiful. But Ernie really gets the credit for that.

Kemp

He possessed the spontaneous vision of a child in his grown-up little boy's room, and it was the child his Hollywood companions loved so much, a vision of life where there was always time. If his advisors understood, they did so grudgingly. When he was supposed to be working on a script done in haste, Moss caught him at the house, in the den building a balsamwood replica of the next wing, "Ferchrissakes, that's what you have architects for," he said. Ernie smiled and continued his infinitely more important project—his playpen.

Ernie had an infectious innocence and enthusiasm for people. At first introduction he immediately wanted to include you in his activities whether it was cigars, cards, steambaths...what's your pleasure? He could confide in you like his long lost Hungarian cousin. He was open to giving away that piece of himself spontaneously. Unfortunately during his lifetime he was copied unmercifully by other comedians who never really understood just how free his laughter was. Close friends tried to protect him, "He was an easy mark and everybody picked his brain, took advantage of him, stole him blind," said Barry Shear, "it would just make his friends sick to watch, but Kovacs was too nice a guy to complain. Most of the unnice people he met, he met out here 'cause this is a town which cuts you apart." Hollywood, herr Hollywood.

Innocence prevailed. At the time of his death Ernie was also thinking about expanding Eugene into a full-length movie. Eugene, the schlemiel, the poor schnook who looked on, astonished at the incongruities of modern life, a character to whom things happened, a character who searched for wonder—statues kissing, doorknobs falling, tables, and world tilting. Eugene was a character born from life, the idealized Kovacs without the big cigar, the big car, and the turntable in the driveway. Eugene was most memorable because he was without pretentions as Ernie was still that goopy kid from Trenton.

Kovacs was in control of his own myth, even if he tended to lavishly overplay his own imagery...a big man with huge hands, jet black mustache. Marc Connelly in his late Seventies, a gentle survivor of a more elegant literary age, good friend from New York, called him "blithe" like his own associates of the Twenties and Thirties. "I remember the color of Ernie, the nimbus around him—I remember it was so three-dimensional—Ernie had practically no echoes in him—a dear preposterous son-of-a-gun. He erupted as much as he wrote...his laughter was generous laughter."

With all his generosity and good nature he was only intolerant of THE RULES, be they those of sponsors, network executives who attempted to censor his creations, or the government which harried him to death...any organized body of pomp, even the hallowed and restricted New York Athletic Club. When Ernie was living in New York and a member of the club, he decided to invite Shear and Cross over for a steambath after work, "We can't go in there," they said, "we're both Jewish. They won't have us as members." Ernie said he'd take care of it, "I won't go in there unless you come with me." They couldn't refuse him and they were his guests several times. "Just be sure when you walk out of the steamroom you carry a towel in front of you so they won't know you're Jewish," he joked. Though he made light of the incident he was extremely concerned all the same—no organization was too austere, no rules so inflexible which couldn't be bent for his friends...hell THEY let *me* in, didn't they, and I'm Hungarian ferchrissakes.

Pretension in any form drew his wrath, albeit comically. When he was still new to Hollywood ways he once, in the company of Shirley Melner, went to a party at the Bel-Aire mansion of William Getz, a producer who happened to be a well-known art collector (unbeknownst to Ernie). They drove up to this huge mansion with an imposing three-story-high front door and were greeted by a Japanese houseboy. (Ernie just finished remarking to Shirl, "Wanna bet they have a Japanese houseboy?" already giggling.) Getz greeted them after being introduced by Sinatra, who left to attend a benefit, and then ushered them into a huge living room with beautiful paintings on the walls. Neither knew where to look first. Bill and the rest of the party sat down on a couch along the wall while Ern and Shirley occupied two commodious easy chairs in front of the sofa. The lights dimmed, the drapes parted, and down came a movie screen covering the paintings...movietime in Bel-Aire, a local custom which neither of the honored guests understood.

While the credits for an Alfred Hitchcock movie were flashing, both were sinking deeper into the plush of the chairs trying to stifle their giggles at all this pomp and circumstance. After ten minutes passed, Getz solicitously came over to them, "You don't like this? You've seen it? OK?" Presto on came June Allyson and Jimmy Stewart in "Strategic Air Command" which made them giggle more. Finally Ernie excused himself to make a phone call, and when he returned told Shirley to do the same. "But I don't have to make a phone call," she protested.

Just do it.

Over the table where the phone sat was Van Gogh's Self-Portrait, the original. They both realized that the pictures on the walls were equally as real. A preposterous situation...Trenton, New Jersey meets Vincent Van Gogh among the palms. "You had it," he said to Shirl. They approached Getz and Ernie said seriously, "Excuse me, Mister Getz, but do you have any UPA cartoons?" No, said Getz. "Well," Ernie replied deadpan, "we'll have to leave."

After being ushered out by the Japanese houseboy and seated on the steps in front of the imposing three-story doors, they hysterically erupted at what they'd seen and done. Ten minutes later they got into Ernie's car and drove out the driveway...up to another house across the street. Ernie may have been an erratic driver at times (he never really got his license), but Shirley was confused.

"What are we doing here?"

"Let's see what movie they're running in this house," he replied.

Nor was that even the end of it. Getz and Kovacs became better friends, and Getz wound up playing cards in the den like everyone else in Hollywood that Ernie met...everyone else. For those who claim to have known him, even his agent who spent many nights at cards, his circle wasn't strictly limited to those few with the million dollar smiles and reputations. "I don't think that he had a friend that was Joe the Butcher," said Moss with the agent's finality.

Not exactly. Ernie made no differentiations between friends. One of those people who was indispensible to Moss and Edd Henri and Edie in those grim days after the accident was a detective from Beverly Hills police force with whom Ernie used to cruise on occasion, a friend that Lemmon knew about from Ernie but had never met. Ernie was used to riding around in patrol cars, still has some good friends on the Trenton force, Detective Anthony Raywood and Fred Hutchinson, the two patrolmen who chased down his first wife in Newark. At his death he was still in contact with 'Van' Kirk, his old dramatics coach. Closer to form, "Ernie was a crazy nut," said Lemmon, "he was a shotgun rather instead of a bullet. He was here, there and everywhere and into all kinds of different relationships with people."

Actually he enlarged his circles as he went along, and the television viewer was privileged to see it all. People still remember Kovacs and his stunts in Trenton. He still walks down its fog-shrouded streets in the downtown area near the Hildebrecht wrapped in his opera cape. Say the name Kovacs in Philadelphia, eyes light up, smiles form. New York City still has a soft spot for Harvey, the World's Strongest Ant. With his death an era was finished.

His boys however, stuck it out, Andy McKay contacted Trig Lund who was down in San Diego with the news. Trig drove directly to Coldwater Canyon to see what he could do, if anything, for Edie. Haley was down in a bar in Pebble Beach when a newspaper mysteriously was shoved under his nose, he didn't even ask for it. He saw the headlines, "Ernie Kovacs TV Star Killed in Crash"...gimme another he said to the bartender. He continued drinking for eight solid hours while his car was sitting in a ten-dollar-an-hour lot. "I had to do my thing the way I think life and death is." Then he drove to a motel and called Edie.

Shirley was so broken up that she was a wreck for weeks, never even made the funeral. Gene Lukowsky cried—he'd worked with Ernie just a few hours before his death in a sweetening session for an upcoming Special. Pieces of time, frozen action, crumpled fender death—they all remember. As for Kemp, there's still an impact after more than a decade for him and others on the lot, "Haley and I were chatting, he made the comment of people reacting and I remember that it was a personal friend that was lost. I couldn't believe it, it can't be true, it can't be. And yet a president is assassinated, people tend to believe it. Yes it must have happened, gee that's sad, it's a bad thing. But with Ernie, no one wanted to believe it, no it couldn't have happened, couldn't of. It was a bad thing for us."

Even talking about the olive inspired other crew members to reverential awe, continues Kemp, "One guy who didn't work on the show overheard us talking and said, 'You know everytime I pass that corner I really think about Ernie, what a shame.' Yet he didn't work with Ernie and he called him 'Ernie' and he remembers the corner and he remembered the car being a Corvair and yet to me, I don't think people remember that." Some facts are indelible.

No, Ernie's still around if you speak with Perry Cross:

> After many years, we were sitting in a restaurant about two years ago (1971)...suddenly Ernie came up and suddenly, subconsciously we started to hear music coming out of the Muzak of all things to hear, was Solfeggio. Suddenly Barry (Shear) said "Hold it..." and we're talking about Ernie. It was like weirdness, beyond

coincidence it was more like somebody was saying, "Hey guys, I know you're talking about me" and that was his little joke on us. It took me about three days to get over that.

One knows instinctively that wherever Ernie is at this moment there is a game in progress with plenty of Havanas and fountains of Jack Daniels and Wild Turkey...sky's the bottom line. It's a good game now, Aristophanes, Ben Johnson, Petronious, Ernie, and Moliere. It's been quite a heavy game, even in these straightened times. Johnson is trying to sucker Ernie into betting, Ernie's got a pair of threes, "Raise ya Ben, just to keep ya honest," he smirks behind his mustache. Meanwhile Sam Goldwyn, Max Sennett, and Harry Cohn mosey over to kibbitz. Moliere has already told Ern that he didn't consider his performance in *L'Avare* hammiest in the least. Johnson agrees, Ben, not Sam.

Maybe not, maybe there's just this huge control room where Ernie is taping, up to his eyes in monitors. He's not laughing exactly, he's sort of smiling after all it was for real, like the photographer said:

He would do a skit and it would be funny but he was serious about it...We all laughed but it was a serious thing to him who wanted to make us laugh.

ACKNOWLEDGEMENTS

At this time I would like to thank those people who aided me in the completion of this book—without them, *Nothing in Moderation* would have remained an idea.

In Trenton, New Jersey: the staff of the Trentonian who welcomed me with open arms, gave me a desk and allowed me to peruse the morgue at my leisure; Ed Hatrak and Edna Vine for the cake, coffee, and interviews; Sam Jacobs; J. Walter Schnorbus; Albert Mathesius for bending the rules a bit; W. Coe McKeeby for undertaking more than a couple of wild goose chases through the State court system; John A. Schaff and Barbara Schaff, my brother-in-law and sister for their hospitality on cold winter nights.

In Philadelphia, Pennsylvania: Ms. Geri Duclow, curator of the Theatre Collection of the Free Library of Philadelphia, for her invaluable aid in tracking down stray articles; Mr. Harry Harris from the *Philadelphia Inquirer* for some of his old Kovacs columns.

In New York City, New York: I thank Harriet Van Horne, a truly elegant lady for her reflections; Marc Connelly; Ken McCormick, Editor-in-Chief at Doubleday and Company who provided me with invaluable letters from his files; Vincent Sardi, Jr., and Martyn, the headwaiter at Sardis, for the lunch and the chat; Rex Lardiner who I hope likes this book; Tom Loeb at CBS for the leads; Shirley Mellner; Jack Mogulescu for his musings on the olive and Dutch Masters for the loan of his clipping book; to Abu Ben Gaiti and "Rizz" at Channel 5; to the Lincoln Center Library of the Performing Arts Theatrical Collection, whose material is invaluable for any researcher in theater and television.

In Los Angeles, California: the Trustees of the University of California at Los Angeles for their permission to quote material from the Kovacs Special Collection; James V. Mink, head of Special Collections; Brooke Whiting, curator of rare books and manuscripts; Hilda Bohem, head of Public Services who cheerfully responded to my queries and helped me preserve Ernie's records with good folders 'borrowed' from the Music department; and Miles Knudsen, Library Assistant for being there when I occasionally went amok.

I owe my thanks as well to Marvin Moss for the good leads and candor in seeing Hollywood for what it really is; to Jack Lemmon for his time and thoughts; to the crews at ABC who gave unstintingly of their energy; to Bob Kemp for his photos; to Bob Haley for the beers; to Bobby Hughes for the script; to Gene Lukowsky; in the 'front office': Ed Henry from Universal, Milt Hoffman, Marianne Hooper from NBC, Joe Behar, Perry Cross, and of course my favorite maverick Barry Shear.

To Edie Adams, a special debt of gratitude for her patience with me and for her foresight in providing not only myself but future students of comedy in general, and Ernie in particular, with a gift of his papers, scripts, and assorted memorabilia to the Special Collections Department Graduate Library at UCLA. Anyone can see them now.

At this time, I wish to thank Katy Hunt for the space in her livingroom at Honey Drive, Laurel Canyon, where I worked and transcribed for the summer of 1973; to Tandy Brodey, my good friend, who got me the space, gave me her companionship and the use of her car; to all the other inhabitants of Honey Drive who helped make that time magical in my life; to Francie Schwartz...again.

I also owe a special debt of gratitude to Andy McKay, a prince among men who not only provided me with a solid chronology of Ernie's early years of Philadelphia and New York television but who also introduced me to Mary Lou Cassidy whose insightful and informative chapter from her uncompleted Masters dissertation on Ernie served as the basis for my own third chapter. I wish to thank her for her Texas encouragement in the face of despair and her correspondence which answered many other questions.

In the final analysis it was the spirit of Ernie which made all my interviews and discussions so rewarding, which motivated me to pursue this project to its inevitable conclusion. I hope he's pleased.

7th Street
New York City
Oct, 1974

APPENDIX

(insert for Kovacs on music....from original script...called "Cartoon") Kovacs on Music, May 22, 1959

The idea, as I explained on the phone, is something Edie has wanted to do for a long time. I once did a thing in Phillie where I was electronically matted into an old Karloff film...We necessarily has (sic) to put me in dark areas in this but the thing worked quite well...This one, of course, be much better. I imagine there will be a little trouble around neckline matchings...There will be two figures cartooned and animated, without heads, so that Edie's and my head can be inserted into these spots camera-wise...This sheet might only be a one and a half minute type thing...

I think the neck line might be best white and if the actual joining spot was not too defined, the live figure...that is the top line of the animated figure meeting the bottom line of the live figure...if this line were rather vague, mistakes in operation might work better....(see A) also...I think the neck would be all animation and the only thing supplied is the head by the live cameras...I think the joining of the head and animation will be easier if the outside edges of the neck don't have to be matched...I must apologize for what seems like a great deal of reiteration (sic), but working through the mail like this, I want to be sure...Let us say we start the whole thing this way...

ERNIE KOVACS 225

...A figure of a girl in a cowgirl outfit (this and opening should make this, all in all, approximately a two and a half or three minute bit) and a figure of a man in cowboy outfit...enter...they do not have heads...The girl opens a small box and takes out a folded guitar which she snaps out large for the box, conceivable, in at least, happy cartoon land, this guitar could, with imagination (be) folded several times to fit into this size box...then male figure going rapidly through his pockets, pulls out small balloon type thing which he blows up and it becomes bass instrument. He has been blowing it up through one of the little gadgets that adjust the string, ties a knot in this and quickly strums a little progression on the strings...He stamps his foot, one and two and one and two...then with gesture prevents guitar player from beginning...exits, returns with two boxes marked his and hers...they open the boxes and each puts on a head, cartoon but as photographically realistic as possible of Kovacs and Adams...facing front, with eyes closed...he outs Kovacs head on girl's body and Edie's on his...she feels above her (no cigar in Kovacs mouth...in drawing) white cowboy hat on each...These hats will have to be copied from the costume department...So...

...ask Marvin Moss at MCA to please have wardrobe immediately get those two hats so that you can duplicate them in your drawing...my size 7 3/8 ask Mary to get Edie to give him hers...So these two drawings of Edie and me are as photographic as possible...

Correction: Edie's facing front, I will face rear Kovacs figure puts up hand, feels Edie's face and hair, snaps finger at Edie's figure and they change places, taking their instruments with them...after check if proper head is in place, discovers that his head is on backwards by feeling in hair as if searching for nose, puts up both hands, turns around facing front...he does too quickly and head starts to slip off, so he straightens it...after this, both figures slap the sides of their own faces vigorously and here is where you take out both heads and camera will put our live heads in place...we slowly open eyes and note we have live heads with cartoon bodies...AFTER SLAPPING PROCESS THE FIGURES ARE DRAWN WITHOUT HEADS UNLESS OTHERWISE NOTED...while this has taken two hours to read, from the beginning to this point should not be too long...perhaps a half a minute, or at most 45 seconds...Now we begin with Kovacs figure beating time with foot to begin song...he stomps a one and two and a one and two...and they begin playing...the other part of the work we will use poetic license on for their existence and they will be heard but not seen...In fact, let us establish them...Let the Kovacs figure point off right when he does, we will heat an "A" on the piano...then he tries, gets a clinker, "A" will sound three or four times more impatiently and firmly until he tunes to position.

Try to do this in positive movements inasmuch as head movements by Kovacs will have to be synched with this action...Costumewise, the two figures' clothing should have humor...perhaps a big gun that weighs heavily on one side and tends to pull trousers down a bit so that Kovacs figure hikes it up now and then...perhaps on Edie's figure, a gun belt that is two (sic) large and whole thing begins sliding down over skirt and she occasionally pulls up...Actually this same device should not be used on both...something different for Edie...And even so, the less number of times this happens, the better unless something really funny can be developed...After Kovacs stomps the one and a two, one and a two, Edie begins singing...she sings:

When I was young I used to wait
On my master and give him his plate
and pass the bottle when he got dry
and brush away the blue tail fly...

ERNIE KOVACS 227

WE IMMEDIATELY HEAR SHRILL WHISTLE, kovacs and edie stop playing and look (physically-live, that is) down to the lower left (camera right) frame...in walks a blue tail fly wearing white tie, top hat and tails...somehow we indicate (even though we are in black and white) that the tails are blue...he is wearing white gloves and carrying cane...he gestures and two flies in stagehands outfits, hammer hooked in belt, etc...come rushing in and plant in the center large pitcher of buttermilk...one runs off, returns quickly with a bag of peanuts which he empties into buttermilk...valet replaces these two and helps formally dressed fly to remove his tails, etc...leaving him in striped shorts...bathing trunks...blue round spot on rear...NOTE: AFTER WE ESTABLISH FORMALLY COATED BLUETAIL FLY ON WHISTLE AND WE SEE EDIE AND ERNIE LOOK DOWN, WE WILL UNTIL INDICATED, NOW USE A DRAWING ONLY OF LOWER SECTION OF LEGS AND POSSIBLY HIPS OF TWO DRAWN FIGURES SO THAT WE CAN SEE THE ACTION OF THE BUTTERMILK BUSINESS CLOSER...A SCRIPT FOR CAMERA WILL BE PREPARED FOR THIS FILM AND HERE THE INDICATION WILL BE FOR CAMERA TO TAKE OUT FACES...after fly props are set and the valet leaves, he snaps finger and we hear EDIE AND ERNIE SONG, BUT DO NOT SEE THEM EXCEPT LOWER EXTREMITIES,

FLIES IN THE BUTTERMILK GOOBER PEAS
FLIES IN THE BUTTERMILK GOOBER PEAS
FLIES IN THE BUTTERMILK GOOBER PEAS

During the singing (a three times repeat of this), the fly runs center takes a quick bow, jumps in the buttermilk the "flies in the buttermilk" line and pulls out two peanuts from the buttermilk on each "goober peas" line...immediately after the last, he flies to his original spot which is quickly set up with a folding director's chair by the little fly stagehand and sits down...THERE IS A STOP IN THE MUSIC WHILE HE DOES THIS, BUT IT MUST BE DONE VERY QUICKLY...he then gestures royally up toward us and we return to the original wide shot...NOTE: IN THE SCRIPT FOR CAMERA, IT WILL NOT BE IN-DICATED KOVACS AND EDIE IN

EDIE SINGS:

I know an old lady, who swallowed a fly...

C.U. FLY WHO DOES A TREMENDOUS TAKE AND DASHES BEHIND CHAIR....SCRIPT: KO-VACS AND EDIE OUT...EDIE SINGS OFF CAM-ERA: PERHAPS SHE'LL DIE...FOR THIS LINE, we either have the fly looking very pleased that the woman will die or sneering at the assumption that a fly could kill her. Which ever look comes off best...or perhaps we have him sneering and looking tough at the thought he could kill an old lady....(LINES NOS. 10 and 11)

AGAIN RETURN TO OUR FULL SHOT...SCRIPT
INDICATES KOVACS AND EDIE *IN*...(no. 12) EDIE
SINGS AND WHEN HE'D RIDE IN THE AF-
TERNOON, I'D FOLLOW WITH A HICKORY
BROOM THE PONY BEING RATHER SHY,
WHEN BITTEN BY THE BLUETAIL
FLY...AGAIN FOR LINES 16, 17, 18 ACTION AS
BEFORE ON CLOSER VIEW OF FLY AND BUT-
TERMILK, SCRIPT INDICATES KOVACS AND
EDIE *OUT*...AFTER LAST LINE THE FLY IS
RATHER WINDED, RETURNS TO HIS CHAIR
PUFFING A BIT, VALET COMES OUT WITH A
GLASS OF SCOTCH AND ICE AND SQUIRTS
SELTZER IN IT...MUSIC IS STOPPED DURING
THIS, FLY GESTURES AND EDIE SINGS LINES
19 and 20...SHE SINGS THIS WHILE WE ARE
STILL ON FLY GEST A LITTLE ON THE
MAL DE MER SIDE FROM THE THOUGHT OF
THIS WOMAN SWALLOWING A SPI-
DER...NOTE:
ON THE FULL SHOTS, THEY MUST ALWAYS BE
THE SAME SIZE AS WE CANNOT CHANGE SIZE OF
FACES...
RETURN TO THE FULL SHOT FOR LINES 21,
22, 23, 24...SCRIPT EDIE AND ERNIE IN...ON
THESE LINES, MUSIC AND EDIE MUST BE
NOTIFIED, THEY WILL BE DONE RATHER
CLASSICALLY WITH SWEEPING VIOLINS AND
COWBOY OUTFIT WILL ABRUPTLY CHANGE
TO EVENING DRESS FOR EDIE AND TAILS FOR
ERNIE...BASS WILL CHANGE TO VIOLIN FOR
KOVACS AND GUITAR WILL BECOME HARP
FOR ADAMS, JUST ON THESE LINES 21, 22, 23,
and 24...

Kovacs and Adams out

THEN RETURN TO OUR FLY SHOT...WHO IS
JUST FINISHING HIS HIGHBALL...HE IS A
LITTLE BAGGED NOW...AND WE HAVE SOME
LITTLE BUBBLES OR SOMETHING ABOVE
HIM TO SHOW HIS DRUNKENNESS AND IN-
DICATIONS AROUND THE EYES AND NOSE...
eyes and nose...
EDIE AND ERNIE SING OFF CAMERA
FLIES IN THE BUTTERMILK (lines 25, 26, and
27...IN THE MIDDLE OF LINE 25 FLY TRIES TO
GET UP, CAN'T MAKE IT, MANAGES TO GET
OVER TO PITCHER ON LINE 26 AND FINALLY
DOES A FAIRLY GOOD THOUGH DRUNKEN
TIME STEP OBVIOUSLY BECAUSE HE CAN-
NOT CLIMB INTO THE PITCHER WITH THE
BUTTERMILK AND GOOBER PEAS BIT...
WE WILL CHANGE LINES TO ORIGINAL FOR
LINES 29, 30...INSTEAD OF CHEESE AND RYE,
IT WILL BE "I KNOW AN OLD LADY WHO
SWALLOWED A HORSE (WHILE ON C.U. OF
FLY) WHO IMMEDIATELY SAYS "RIDI-
CULOUS" AND THE LINE FOLLOWS THAT IS
"SHE'S DEAD OF COURSE"...AFTER THIS LINE
WIDE SHOT WITH ALL THREE DOING A TIME
STEP FOR ABOUT FOUR FAST BARS AS A FIN-
ISH TO MUSIC...THEY DO A TYPICAL VAUDE-
VILLIAN FINISH. THE STAMP TO THE RIGHT
FOOT AND THE RIGHT HAND OUT TO AC-
KNOWLEDGE APPLAUSE AND HERE WE GO
OUT OF FILM...

The following is going to be either the downfall of us technically or at least mentally.

Here are the instructions for the construction and various little activities regarding what we will call the "Jealousy" bit. We're going to shoot it in three sections- this is to offset using a million extra people and also to make it somewhat easier as this is a particularly difficult thing to handle technically where there are going to be many willing hands fumbling the shit out of this one including my own. Look at it this way: This is the last one of the four and if everything goes well, I may turn down the proposition to do twelve (wouldn't that be a kick in the ass!) next year.

I am attaching to this the drawings:

Drawing No. 1-

You will see a water cooler upstage. This is very deceptive. It is more than a water cooler. In front of the water cooler is a typewriter on a stand. In back of the water cooler is a clock. On top of the clock is a little black bird. (This is the little rubber black bird that works with the rubber ball. I'll show it to you and I think we should get a million of them in case they go bad. I think 6 really ought to do it. See, I remembered the budget.)

The table holding the typewriter must be high enough so that the roller on the typewriter is a couple of inches above the metal part of the water cooler. In other words, a couple of inches on to the lower part of the glass. The typewriter must have four keys that can work by remote control. They will work- one, two, three- one, two, three- one, two, three, four (I believe that's the correct order...the fourth key is only used once at the end.) The others go in succession- left to right, right to left, left to right and the fourth one. The water cooler must have two separate working effects that can be worked completely under control. Water spout must shoot out water in spurts, under control, and we must have an air hose that can start bubbles at the bottom of the glass water cooler, either in short spurts or long streams.

The clock is a fairly fast moving clock and must move completely in time with the music. I think you'll find that the pendulum on the clock swings about two times to the second. The little bird will be worked by a rubber ball...this is all up against the wall as you can see from the drawing. The clock should be located on the wall so that the lower rim of the clock is about an inch below the top rim of the glass cooler. On the center of the clock, at the top, is where the little black bird is located. Use a medium gray wall on this set.

To the stage left of this is a filing cabinet. There are three drawers, medium, and the bottom drawer should be larger. These drawers must be able to be worked individually from the back as you would a slide trombone. Fake it with a little paper inside as though they were filled. The bottom drawer could be empty, but paint it black inside. The bottom drawer must also work like a slide trombone and at the end will slide something like six feet, or eight even, if we can.

To the left of this is a radiator...at the end of the bit, the very end of the bit, we must have a good spout of steam come out of the valve. The valve should be located stage *right* of the radiator. In other words, it is on the stage right side of the radiator which locates it between the filing cabinet and the radiator. To stage left of the radiator is a switchboard. And if you think you had trouble-wait till you read this: We should get a switchboard with approximately 6 rows of lights, *if possible*. These must be able to work as we want them. The main effect will be starting at the top left row and going all the way to the end of that row and starting at right of the second row and going all the way to the left of the second row, starting at the left of the third row and going all the way to the right of the third row, starting at the right of the fourth row and going and going to the left of the fifth row and so forth. In other words, it comes down snakelike...a kind of backward "s" design all the way down. The keys that are flipped on this board should be painted white so that they can be seen and I would like to be able to work them either individually, and- or as a group (manually). There should be four of the line connectors (the long cords that are stuck into the board- they should be painted a light gray color, and they must be made to flip back and fourth. I will describe that a little better. If they are slightly bowed and can be made to sway in unison, that is the effect we want. If it also can be added that we can push them out from the back at the end, that would be helpful.

The desk, which is stage right of the water cooler (disregarding the top of the desk which is REALLY complicated) must have the drawers in this manner: Facing the desk and starting at the lower left side, I would like the drawers to go open in succession, bottom left first, next one next, top left next, center top next, right top next, and the other two in that same order, and then reverse and have them close in the same order. The top of the desk is where we get complicated.

And now we can see Drawing No. 2 for this one:
I do not think that the width of the desk should be too much, but I would suggest no less than three feet. Facing the desk on the lower left hand corner is a large old fashioned fountain pen, lying on a large white sheet of paper, preferably three or four sheets of paper-blank. In time to the music, this pen must drop gobs of ink out of the point. The phone which will be located directly in back of the pen must have the dial work briefly only one full turn will be needed in syncronization to the music in short movements, a kind of syncopated beat, the ear-piece and talking-piece of the phone must be made to rock back and forth in time to the music while remaining on the cradle it raises on one end, drops, raises on the other end, and drops sort of a banjo effect but also must be completely controlled manually. To the right of the phone is an old fashioned pencil sharpener, with the hole facing us. I would like a little electric motor to turn the handle on this which will be at the back, but the

handle should be big enough so that when we see it facing the hole-end we can still see the end of the handle going around in the back. Directly in back of this is the water carafe with a large thermos-type cork stuck on top. This must be made to raise and lower on musical cue. I would suggest that the cork be about 4 inches long so that we can push it up as high as that much and lower it again. (Again facing the desk) to the right of this carafe are four water glasses. These must be able to be tapped from the bottom so that they will move, visibly. On the lower right end of the desk is a desk spindle which is possibly the most interesting device on the desk. This should have three sheets of paper approximately 5 by 7 with some scribbling on it attached at equal distance places on the spindle. I would like this to work in this manner that the spindle can be pulled into the desk, pushed up again and the pieces of paper will resume their original position. The spindle should be about eight inches high but also capable of going another twelve inches up for effect. At limbo, I would like ten paper clips on what appears to be a tray. The effect that I would like on this tray (and remember it is at limbo) is for us to draw a magnet beneath the tray causing the ten paper clips to pile up at the end, but they must pile up individually and I would humbly suggest that a small series of ridges such as a folded piece of heavy paper laid out with the paper clips placed on the side of the ridge so that when the magnet is drawn from the right to the left, the paper clips will not go over the ridge. However, they will go off at the other end. This is much in the manner of some shallow steps. Picturing this as a shallow stairway with the paper clips in each one and a magnet drawn from the top of the stairs to the bottom, the paper clips could not physically go up the steps to meet the magnet, but as the magnet passed underneath it would gather each of the paper clips to pile up on the bottom step. As we are going to shoot this in sections, let us discuss manpower.

(manpower disquisition)

In order to save some money on this, we will shoot this in sections rather than as a whole. Therefore, we can have some people double on instruments, as the expression goes. We will need two people working the filing cabinet...at the water cooler the clock can be on a motor but the bird will be operated manually, the typewriter will be operated manually and the water cooler will be operated manually. However, the typewriter will be operated and then we will lift the camera off it, so whoever is operating the typewriter can also work the water cooler. When we are on the bird that will be operating all by itself. also...so I leave it to you to work this out as best you can.

Later, at the water cooler, there is one thing that I forgot to discuss above...there is a papercup dispenser beside it. Four times (two times each, each two in close succession to the other) I need a whole zing of papercups to shoot out. They can come out disjointed, or they can come out in one long stream it doesn't matter...if it's easier in one long stream we'll do it that way. The paper clips, of course, we'll need one man to operate and if it will help any we can shoot that as an insert. The switchboard we'll need one person operating the lights, one person operating the keys. The person operating the keys can also operate the cables. The desk in this first sequence, we'll need the operation of the seven drawers opening in that sweeping "U" turn, and then closing in that sweeping "U" turn. And that is our problem. I would like Bobby Hughes to work the water cooler, certainly, the bird, and the typewriter. The stuff that is on top of the desk will be shot separately so that the same people operating that can operate the top of the desk. On top of the desk I would like Bobby to work the fountain pen and the glasses and anything else that he can operate from there. The pencil sharpener can be worked on an electric switch and the bottom turned on to have the handle revolve when we need it and will not require attention. Your big problem obviously, will be in grouping this stuff so that it can be operated and still have those drawers operating. Consequently, someone obviously underneath the desk. I suggest a fake backing for the knee hole section so that someone can actually sit there and work these things. If it is necessary to group

them more towards the center than I have indicated, we can do that.
I don't know how the hell you're going to get this done by Sunday- but "rots of ruck."

Ernie (with love)

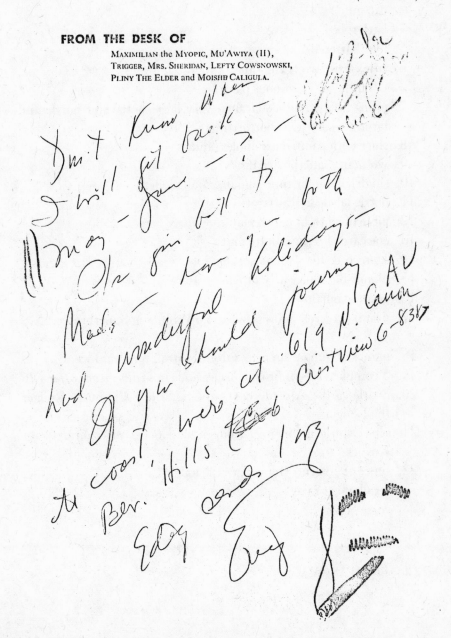

FROM THE DESK OF
Maximilian the Myopic, Mu'Awiya (II), Trigger, Mrs. Sheridan, Lefty Cowsnowski, Pliny The Elder and Moishe Caligula.

Dec. 30, 1952....prop list

1. cigar with long thread
2. wooden watch with long thread
3. cap gun
4. bath robe
5. hat (battered)
6. title cards: wolfgang sauerbraten
       on the air (luminous paint)
7. props for pfffif (deodarant)- very large hot water bottle and large economy size bottle (trig)
8. shirt with painted arm holes (andy)
9. wolfgang sauerbraten (andy)
10. single chime for time signal...small mellet
11. bottle labeled: Raus mit: (trig)
12. piece of cloth to polish piano
13. cue cards for sauerbraten bit
14. 15 records for the sauerbraten bit
15. blonde pig tailed wig for edie
16. german outfit
17. postal card: on address side: To Wolfgang Sauerbraten CBS T.V. N.Y.
18. names of hungarian pieces from Hatrak for clearance
19. 5 complete sets of broken dishes and cups (*silverware offer-ed*)
20. 2 title cards: Already drawn (Trig, Lady Flatbush, Rodger the Lodger)
21. sep script large print of Rodger the Lodger offer on desk for Kovacs
22. super of 43 cents (for rodger the lodger)
      1 roll of car tape
      corset stays

pound of window putty on dish
one doz. frankfurters, linked
candlelabra
marshmellow sunday in dish
table cloth

23. four local phone numbers
    four out of town phone numbers
    same as above written out for kovacs to be read
24. sheets for tonsorials barber shop quartet song
25. towel, hot and shaving cream and brush for lather (rise) cup,
    razor
26. costumes for two barbers and two customers
27. the hatrak barber show with winter garb on it: old fashioned
    winter coat and garb...sauerbraten' coat can be used and a
    couple of derbys
28. pic of dad dovetonsils
29. costume for percy, cigarette holder and cigarette
30. script large type of trig lund for razor bit
31. 3 cards: Look Sharp, feel sharp, *cut yourself*
32. baseball outfit for kovacs
33. dope wig
34. 7 or 8 pieces of metal about three inches long
35. safety razor
36. box of bandaids for Ed Hatrak
37. *Note: Russ must be notified for all sound effects to be used
    tuesday night*
38. divers helmet
    large anchor
    tank with water and hose: (there are for super on where you
    do worka john
39. cards, title for where do you worka john, prize book, and desk
    sign
40. foop bottle (see trig: filled with powder)
41. large type script for trigger
42. script for K where do you worka john
43. measles card and filter, and cut out figure (see trigger)

ERNIE KOVACS   239

TELEVISION BACKGROUND with ERNIE KOVACS in
New York -
from April 21, 1952 to January 1957.

1 - "KOVACS UNLIMITED" - (As an Assoc. Producer)
WCBS-TV, Local
12:45-1:30 PM, Mondays to Friday,
   April 21 to Dec. 26, 1952.
8:30-9:30 AM, Monday to Friday,
   Dec. 29, 1952 to July 5, 1953.
8:00-9:00 AM, Monday to Friday,
   July 8, 1953 to Jan. 15, 1954
      (NOTE: While the above show was on the air - another
         show was inaugurated, namely, the following:)

2 - "THE ERNIE KOVACS SHOW" - ·
CBS-TV Network (opposite Milton Berle on NBC-TV)
8:00-9:00 PM, Tuesdays, Dec. 30, 1952 to April 14, 1953.

3 - "THE ERNIE KOVACS SHOW" -
WABD (Dumont TV) - Local
11:15 PM to 12:15 AM, Monday to Friday,
   April 12, 1954 to Jan. 7, 1955
10:30 to 11:00 PM, Tuesdays and Thursdays,
   Jan. 11 to Feb. 24, 1955
10:00 to 11:00 PM, Tuesdays and Thursdays,
   March 1 to April 7, 1955 (NOTE: This last 1 hour show
         was called "THE ERNIE KOVACS RE-
         HEARSAL".)

4 - ABC-Radio's "TONIGHT" -
NBC-TV Network
11:00 PM to 1:00 AM, Mondays and Tuesdays
   November 1956 to January 1957
   Oct. 1, '56 - Jan. 22, '57

Apr. 21 '52-Jan. 15, '54 (8:00)
Kovacs Unlimited (local)

Jan. 6-Apr. 14, '53 (8-9 PM)
The Ernie Kovacs Show

Mar. 5-July 2, '54
I'll Buy That-panelist

June 6, 1955   Person-to-Person (guest)

July 21, 1957   Ed Sullivan Show

July 27, 1958   Ed Sullivan Show

Sept. 26, 1957   Playhouse 90-*Topaze* (stars)

June 6, 1958   The Big Record (Gen.Mtrs)-guest

October 19, 1958 GE Theater-*The World's Greatest
                  Quarterback*-(Sam Lund)

February 2, 1959 Westinghouse/Desilu Playhouse-
                  Symbol of Authority-(Arthur Witten)

February 15, 1959
GE Theater-*I was a Bloodhound*   Barney Colby
June 14, 195   (rerun)
April 1, 1960   Westinghouse/Lucille Ball/Desi Arnez
                  Show-guest appearance

March 8, 1961   US Steel Hour-*Private Eye, Private Eye*

Radio

November 3, 1957
Mitch Miller Show

September 9, 1956
Mitch Miller Show

August 5, 1957   This is New York

Mar. 7-Mar. 9, '51
It's Time for Ernie (Phila)

May 14-June 29, '51
Time for Ernie (Phila)

July 2-Aug. 24, '51
Ernie in Kovacsland (Phila)

Sept. 20, 1951   guest panalist
(WNBT)   VIM Electric "Quick on the Draw"

Sept. 2, 1951   guest panalist
(WNBT)   VIM Electric "Vim Talent Search"

Sept. 30, 1951   guest judge
(WNBT)   VIM Electric

Oct. 11, 1951   VIM Electric "Quick on the Draw"

Jan. 7, 1951-Mar. 28, 1952
                   Kovacs on the Corner (Phila)
(Network)   (features folks who frequent Kovacs' alley)

April 27, 1955   Tonight (Steve Allen host)-guest

June 24, 1955   Tonight (Steve Allen host)-guest

Aug. 29-Sept. 13, 1955
                   Tonight (substitute for Allen)

Dec. 9, 1955   Tonight - guest

**Dec. 12, 1955-July 27, 1956
                   The Ernie Kovacs Show
                   10:30-11:00 AM Mon.-Fri.

Dec. 7, 1955   Home (guest interviewed)

Dec. 9, 1955   Today (guest interviewed)

*Jan. 15, 1956   NBC Comedy Hour (featured guest)

July 1, 1956   Steve Allen Show - guest

**July 2-Sept. 10, 1956
The Ernie Kovacs Show (repl. Caesar)

Sept. 28, 1956   Today (horticulture sketch w/Garroway)

Sept. 21, 1956   It Could Be You - guest

Oct. 5, 1956   Walter Winchell Show

**Oct. 1, 1956-Jan. 22, 1957
                 Tonight (M & Tu night alternate with Allen W-F)

Nov. 22, 1956   Parades 1956-Macy's Thanksgiving Parade

Dec. 9, 1956
March 30, 1957   Wide Wide World - film commercial
May 12, 1957   with Edie Adams for GM
June 9, 1957

Dec. 22, 1956   Saturday Color Carnival-(The Sonja Henie Ice Spectacular)

Feb. 23, 1956   The Perry Como Show

***Jan. 19, 1957 Saturday Color Carnival-*The Ernie Kovacs Show* - silent show
(half hour repl. for Jerry Lewis)

Feb. 16, 1957   Saturday Color Carnival-TV Emmy Show (performs)

Feb. 15, 1957   Tonight! America After Dark via switch to Hawaiian Rm.,
                 Lexington Hotel (NY)

March 16, 1957   Saturday Color Carnival-Academy Awards TV

March 31, 1957   Wide Wide World-"Spring Jubilee" from Beverly Hills
                 Hotel (remote pickup of fashion show)

May 27, 1957   Producers' Showcase-Festival of Magic-emcee

ERNIE KOVACS   243

May 20, 1957   Truth or Consequences-guest participant

August 20, 1957 Tex and Jinx Show-guest interview

July 26, 1957   Tonight! America After Dark-interview with wife in NYC apartment

Nov. 10, 1957 Wide Wide World-"The Fabulous Infant", does silent comedy bit on kine and appears *live* talks about career in TV

Oct. 23, 1957 Today-interview on book "Zoomar"

Oct. 26, 1957 Perry Como Show-guest

Oct. 5, 1957   Max Factor - The Polly Bergen Show-guest

Oct. 29, 1957 Bride & Groom-special guest

Nov. 24, 1957 Dinah Shore Chevy Show-guest

Dec. 31, 1957 George Gobel Show-guest

Dec. 20, 1957 Truth or Consequences-guest

June 18, 1958 Today-film (5:05) of K getting haircut for movie role

Oct. 16, 1958 Ford Division, For Motor-The Ford Show (Tennessee Ernie Ford)-guest

Sept. 30, 1958
Feb. 15, 1959 Eddie Fisher Show

Apr. 6, 1959   "Oscar Show"

**May 22, 1959 Kovacs on Music

Oct. 6, 1959   Ford Motor-Ford Startime-"The Wonderful World of Entertainment"-guest

Dec. 11, 1959 Buick-Bob Hope Buick Show-guest

**Apr. 11, 1960   Goodyear Tire and Rubber Co.-"Goodyear Theater stars as Maximilian Krob in *Author at Work* (Durrenmatt)

Feb. 22, 1961   Here's Hollywood

May 22, 1962   14th Annual Emmy Emmy Awards-tape of scene from one of specials and tape of scene from "Laughter USA"

Radio

July 22-25, 1957   Nightline-tape narrated, this series called Hungarian "White Paper"-a study of this important document quoting from essential texts and using actual NBC News broadcasts of that period (Hungarian Revolt)

Mar. 31, 1958   Groucho Marx - guest

The Films of Ernie Kovacs

Name (Company	Release Date	Director	Actors
Operation Madball (Columbia)	1957	R. Quine	Jack Lemmon, Mickey Rooney Arthur O'Connell, Kathryn Grant, E. Kovacs
Bell, Book and Candle (Columbia)	1959	R. Quine	James Stewart, Kim Novak Jack Lemmon, E. Kovacs Hermione Gingold, Janice Rule, Elsa Lancaster
It Happened to Jane (Columbia)	1959	R. Quine	Doris Day, Jack Lemmon, E. Kovacs
Our Man in Havana (Columbia)	1960	Carol Reed	Alec Guiness, Burl Ives, Maureen O'Hara, Noel Coward, Ralph Richardson, Jo Morrow, E. Kovacs
Strangers When We Meet (Columbia)	1960	R. Quine	Kirk Douglass, Kim Novak, Barbara Rush, E. Kovacs
Wake Me When It's Over (Fox)	1960	Mervyn Leroy	Jack Warden, Dick Shawn, Margot Moore, E. Kovacs
North to Alaska (Fox)	1960	Henry Hathaway	John Wayne, Fabian, Stewart Granger, Capucine, Mickey Schaunessy, E. Kovacs
Five Golden Hours (Columbia)	1961	Mario Zampi	Cyd Charisse, George Saunders, E. Kovacs
Sail a Crooked Ship (Columbia)	1962	Irving Brecher	Robert Wagner, Delores Hart, Carolyn Jones, E. Kovacs

MY TELEVISION BACKGROUND with ERNIE KOVACS in Philadelphia, Pa.
from March 20, 1950 to April 18, 1952 on WPTZ (Local and NBC)

_____ 1950   _____ 1951   _____ 1952

"DEADLINE FOR DINNER," Local, sponsored Cooking Show, 2-2:30 PM, twice a week,
March 20, 1950 to April 18, 1952.

"THREE TO GET READY," Local, sponsored Variety show,
Monday to Friday, Nov. 27, 1950 to March 28, 1952. Nov. 27,
1950 to Sept. 14, 1951, 7:30 to 9 AM; Sept. 17, 1951 to
March 28, 1952, 7 to 9 AM.

"IT'S TIME FOR ERNIE,"
NBC-TV Network Variety Show,
3:15 to 3:30 PM
Monday to Friday,
May 14, 1951 to June 29, 1951

"NOW YOU'RE COOKING,"
Local, sponsored Cooking Show,
2-2:30 PM, once a week,
May 15 to June 12, 1951 and
Sept. 18 to Oct. 16, 1951

"ERNIE IN KOVACSLAND,"
NBC-TV, Network Variety Show,
7-7:30 PM, Monday to Friday
July 2, to August 24, 1951
(Show replaced "Kukla, Fran &
Ollie" for vacation)

"KOVACS ON THE CORNER,"
NBC-TV, Network Variety Show,
11:30 to 12:00 Noon, Monday to Friday
November 1951 to March 1952

Courtesy of Andrew C. McKay